# ABOUT THE AUTHOR

Ciaran Mullooly is RTE Midlands Correspondent and a former winner of the AT Cross National Media Awards and Medical Journalist Of The Year Award.

He has worked in journalism for 30 years, training as a reporter in the Longford Leader, The Cavan Leader and Shannonside Radio. His first TV role was as a reporter with 'Ear To The Ground' on RTE 1.

Ciaran's first book "Death on Holy Thursday - the shooting of John Carthy in Abbeylara' was published by Blackwater Press in November 2006.

In 2015 he researched and presented the acclaimed 'The Longford Phoenix' documentary on RTE television, telling the story of the restoration of St. Mel's Cathedral after a devastating fire in 2009.

Ciaran has also worked as a volunteer in community development throughou_____ Westmeath for more than thirty years, _____ e quality of life and developing r_____ ling Hub, Roscommon Lions Clul_____ rea Mens Shed group, Rathcline (_____ newal & Tidy Towns, Longford County Tourism Committee, the Midland Samaritans Fashion Show at AIT, Lions Clubs International / Lions Clubs of Ireland, Lough Ree Bay Tennis Club, Athlone Lions Club, the Athlone Marconi Heritage committee and the Lough Ree Area Community Co-op & Amenity Groups.

D1437979

# Back
# to the
# Future

*Reflections on rural life, recession
and renewal over 30 years of journalism*

## CIARAN MULLOOLY

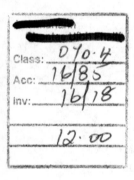
First published in 2015 by Media People Ireland
(Roscommon People), Abbey Street, Roscommon

Copyright Ciaran Mullooly 2015

ISBN: 978-0-9569566-5-1

Cover Photo: www.nicolettespelicphotography.com
Printed by: Turners Printing Company
Design by: Roscommon People

To Angela, Bryan and Eoghan
– the three people on this earth
with whom I share the best of times,
the most special of places
and the greatest of love.

# CONTENTS

# Introduction

At the end of January 2013, I went to see the Head of News & Current Affairs in RTE, Kevin Bakhurst and set out my stall for two new projects I was trying to get kickstarted over the following months. The first was easy, only costing about €30 million to put in place, would involve going to church quite a lot, and would be all over within 23 months. A bit of a Grand Designs, Spiritual Special you might call it. The restoration of St. Mel's Cathedral, Longford was already in full flow. Three years after a devastating fire had closed the building, huge work had gone into planning its rebirth and the first stage of the stabilisation of what remained was well under way. Over the previous twelve months I had talked to everyone involved in the project and discussed the structure of a special one-hour RTE television documentary mapping every key stage of the building work as it was re-shaped. Within a few months, we were in the charred remains of the old cathedral shooting our first images of those famous old limestone columns as they were slowly taken down and replaced.

'The Longford Phoenix' TV documentary was two years in the making and eventually aired to an audience of over half a million people. The reaction from both public and critics was exceptional. Most marvelled at the artistry and elevated skills of the plasterers, labourers and builders on the new cathedral building site and, when it was finished, wondered even more at the beauty that had been created. Alongside the physical changes, the documentary also examined the current state of the faith of the people as well as the church's own journey of rehabilitation following decades of sexual abuse related scandals. The documentary was expertly produced by Birthe Tonseth of the RTE 'Would You Believe' team. Once the cathedral was re-opened and 'Longford Phoenix' went to air, over a hundred thousand people marched up those steps and visited the building within 9 months, making it an important tourism location for the people of Longford, as well as a renewed spiritual home.

The second project I unveiled to Kevin that day was very much a work in progress. It started out with the loose format of 'a waterways book', a collection of tales and yarns surrounding journeys on the majestic river Shannon arising from my investment in an old steel-hulled Dutch motor cruiser in 2004. The plan at the outset was straight-forward: the book would chart the detail and colour of those boat trips north and south and, as we met the many wonderful characters along the route, expand on something we all knew, namely, that this stretch of open waterway was not just the longest in Britain and Ireland but by far the most scenic and interesting too. The formula for the book had already been established in the late 1990's when, upon leaving the 'Ear To The Ground' programme on RTE television and joining the newsroom, this writer began a weekly column in the Roscommon Champion provincial newspaper. Each week I wrote about the boat trips, the rivers, the lakes and the occurrences that went on alongside on the dry land too. There were columns on celebrations, success, politics, nature, history, murder, death and destruction: all human life was there.

It was only last year when I sat down to re-read some of that original work that I realised the vast changes that had taken place in the country since I first started out in journalism three decades ago. The Ireland of 1985 when I worked for the Longford Leader, was very different to the one of our post-bailout nation, and the midland counties of Longford, Westmeath and Roscommon were even more unrecognisable to an author living and working in this region pretty much all the time. This led me to update the original columns and concentrate on some of those changes, reflecting on life here before and during the recession, and then focussing on some of the people who had come and gone in the same era, historical figures in our lifetime, local legends. References for each article can be found at the back of the book. In preparing the text I also began to hone in for the first time on some of the challenges that had surfaced for those living in my home town of Lanesborough and Ballyleague on the river Shannon at the top of Lough Ree, a proud people in a town symbolic of so many more around the country experiencing unemployment, emigration and dereliction as the social and economic movement from country to city advances at pace for so many of our youth.

Today Lanesborough and Ballyleague, like so many other towns of their sizes in rural Ireland, face huge challenges in restoring their commerce and character, but there are very definite indications of new life already emerging, and in this book I try to detail some of the progress made and the options facing the people who live in rural Ireland. Ninety per cent of this 'vision' for the future could easily apply to any other rural town in the country and I hope many of the readers will take back to their own native parishes and towns after reading this book a message that country-people hold their fate in their own hands and possess tons and tons of the only real ingredient needed to change their destiny – perseverance and commitment.

To make sense of it all for readers I have chosen to begin with a biographical note on my own life and times, a guide to the family background and the community into which I was born, the times we lived in and the challenges we faced growing up and seeking employment near Lough Ree. Writing my own memoirs was not part of the plan for this book so what follows is an abbreviated guide to the author and his family. I hope it sets the scene for you, gives an indication of the values I hold dear and will help you to understand where I have come from and the depth of the challenge ahead.

# FROM THERE TO HERE

I was born in Killinure, Lanesborough, County Longford on 4th September, 1966, the son of Daniel Mullooly, a farmer and chain-smoking ex-Rathcline footballer whose passions in life were few but centred mainly on horse-racing like his three brothers at the Turlough Races, Grand Parade cigarettes by the box of twenty and, unusually for a man of his generation, wildlife TV programming, David Attenborough to the forefront.

Dan Mullooly was born in 1914 in a very different Ireland. Times were tough. His mother Annie died when he was only eight years old, also losing two infant sons. He worked hard on the farm, played goalkeeper for his GAA club, had a dodgy knee and retired early from the game. He was also a man with a fierce temper, or rather what my mother called a 'contrariness' that often had its roots in the lack of cigarettes during the weeks of Lent or just had no roots at all. Like his brothers and his parents he worked damn hard throughout his life, much more so than any of his sons ever did, and his life evolved from the land to the bog to the creamery and, from time to time in later years, to a night out with the Kilina Ceili band at John Shiels' pub in Doughill, Curraghroe across the Shannon in the shadow on mighty Sliabh Bawn. His best friend Sonny Shanley from Killashee was usually with him on those musical trips.

My mother was Winifred 'Mollie' Gilleran from Clonkeel, Killashee, County Longford, born in 1922, a woman who studied domestic science and much more at places like St. Brigid's College in Ardagh and the Munster Institute on Model Farm Road in Cork. She also worked in the hotel trade from time to time, regaling us at a later stage in her life with tales of the odd boyfriend and acquaintances as far away as the Royal Hotel in Bangor and several Dublin inns. Like the man she married, she was born on the edge of a bog. The Gilleran's homestead is just a short distance from the river Shannon near Clonbearla in Killashee, but it was the train and horse and trap to Dublin that took away not one but three of her siblings in the tide of emigration as she grew up, and she was very emotionally affected when her three sisters left and set up a new life with jobs in Birmingham. Her brother Tommy was a very intelligent man who won a free scholarship to St. Mel's College in Longford but stayed at home to farm the land in Killashee. He was the only boy in the house and such were the times they lived in. The Gillerans and their neighbours the Killians were joined together by more than land, working with and helping each other on the bog and the farms. My mother's cousin Tommy Killian from Killashee was a firm favourite and great friend and remained so until the day she died.

Mollie Gilleran married at a ridiculously young age, and her mother told her so. I think the tall, dark and handsome Rathcline footballer Daniel Mullooly swept her off her feet a little and, though her mother and others tried to warn her against it, they were joined in matrimony at St. Andrew's Church, Westland Row, Dublin in 1946. She wasn't even 25 years old. My uncle Paddy Mullooly picked them up afterwards from the train station in Longford and brought them home to her new life in Killinure, a small thatched cottage with no toilet which was to become her new centre of life and provide the setting for fifty hard-working years of marriage. Paddy was a a bit of jester in those days and stopped at the ruins of a cow shed down the road some distance from home before announcing to my mother that this broken-down and ramshackle old byre was to be her new home. For a moment she looked a bit worried, he often joked later.

These were tough times in Irish history, occasions of great poverty, hardship and neglect, and Dan and Mollie Mullooly were no different to anyone else struggling to come up with the money to raise a family of three boys and three girls - Nuala, Rose, Eithne, Pat, Donal and myself. Seeing as I wasn't actually born until 1966, I have to rely on my siblings for the exact detail of those difficult years but I have heard the stories of food shortages and hard labour so many times now that it doesn't tend to go away easily. In truth, my mother and father worked incredibly hard on their farm and made outrageous personal sacrifices to raise their family and give us a decent quality of life in Killinure. It is the small things that stick in the memory most when recalling the anecdotes from that period: the sale of eggs to allow my sisters go to a dance on a night out, the rearing of turkeys to pay for Christmas presents, my father's long association with keeping, killing and selling on pigs in the days before a dairy herd emerged as chief paymaster for all of our educations. I was old enough to see the metamorphosis that the same dairy business brought to our house, a shiny new Gascoigne milking machine, a converted parlour and then later a refrigerated bulk-milk tank for the first time. The ever-reliable Paddy Farrell from Newtowncashel took the milk-cans to the creamery and, though the monthly cheque was a decent one, it was also hard work.

Dan Mullooly proudly proclaimed for many years that he was the first farmer in County Longford to make big round bales on the land. I remember the day very well when the strange-shaped green machine from Coolarty near Granard arrived in the field behind our neighbours, the Kenny's homestead, and within minutes the farmers of the parish flocked to see to the commotion of a very big and round bale of green grass emerging into the daylight from the heart of this animal to be followed shortly afterwards by the even more dynamic view of the same bale being wrapped up like a Christmas present in black polythene in a frenzy of activity. A young man called Liam Murray drove the tractor that did the baling and wrapping and later went on to be a priest at St. Mary's Church in Athlone beside the

RTE studio where I worked for many years. I think he's now parish priest in Ballymahon, a far cry from his pioneering work in south Longford agriculture.

It was not an era without tragedy. I grew up with the tale of my father's cousin Dominic Dowd from Carrastrawley losing his life, an occurrence perpetually recalled in our house and especially when we drove the roads around Greenhall in Newtowncashel. The tractor he was driving had apparently turned over on a bend of the road and he was tragically killed at a very young age. Much later, one of the darkest memories of my youth was to return from school one winter's day to be told of the shocking death of my first cousin James Mullooly in an accident in Galway city. A promising young chef, his innocent life was snuffed out instantly in a traffic accident on February 3rd, 1981. It was a blow that pierced the hearts of his parents Mary and Jimmy, shocked all his siblings, and hung around Killinure like a black cloud for years. For some strange reason I have no memory of the funeral itself but can instantly recall the long and torturous journey home from Galway with his remains, standing in the street beside the hearse in places like Mountbellew when the cortege stopped for a while. It was the first experience of personal grief in my life - but unfortunately not the last one.

Attending St. Mary's Boys National School on the Green, Lanesborough was largely uneventful for me, taught as I was by Ms Meehan, Ms Beirne and Master Sean Logue. This followed a period when the school itself had been at the centre of some controversy. Logue was a Kerryman with a passion for football and another who couldn't control his anger. Later in life he was also convicted for a sexual offence with a young pedestrian he gave a lift to along a public road, but during my time in his class I witnessed nothing except his temper in action.

I enjoyed the school on the Green in Lanesborough and made many friends - from both the town and country. There was always a great rivalry but good fun too and many of the students went on to make their own mark in all sorts of ways - none more so than Kip Carroll a friend in first class who hailed from Clonbonny house outside the town, by his own admission lived with dyslexia and found the school difficult, yet went on to become one of the top national newspaper photographers in Ireland.

Logue pushed the brighter students to the very edge of their capability, perhaps some of them too far, and would occasionally beat someone whose only sin was not to know the answer to his question. It was brutal to watch, especially when the assault was prolonged, but fortunately my memory is that it was only on a small number of occasions this happened. We were, however, afraid of him for most of our days in that school, and with good cause.

Many town elders knew well at the time, but I only learned much later, that a previous teacher had left even greater damage in his wake. School principal Donal Dunne taught for forty years, during which time he destroyed the innocence of schoolboys trusted into his care at as many as six schools, including the Boys National School in Lanesborough in the 1950s and 1960. Jailed for two years in 1999 for sexually abusing boys at two midland schools, he admitted committing similar offences in three other schools at Mullingar CBS, County Westmeath, Griffith Avenue and St. James Street, Dublin. His ability to continuously molest children before seamlessly changing jobs and moving to another school to do so again was shocking. In 1966, having worked at and abused children in four schools, and some time following his stay in Lanesborough, it was an appointment to Walsh Island near Tullamore which led to the assaults that ultimately caught up with him in the courts later on. In that small rural Offaly school he proceeded to abuse a number of boys, six of whom courageously later made the statements that brought about his conviction long after he had retired.

I covered that court case in Offaly and learned for the first time of the trail of horror that Dunne had left behind. The failure by parish priests and others to stop and report him to the Gardai allowed Dunne to continue making misery for dozens of schoolboys. He abused and beat several local boys when he was in our school, parting after only a short while but leaving the emotional and physical scars that sexual abuse brings on the lives of so many in the community.

Following national school, I went next-door to Lanesborough Tech in search of a secondary education, not because I had any major 'grá' for technical subjects at this young stage in my life, but mainly because my mother wasn't prepared to spend again on a St. Mel's College education. Mollie Mullooly was nothing if not a practical woman. She knew what she thought best for her son and decided the calibre of the local teaching staff was enough for her youngest son and a final sojourn into 'free' education. She was also trying to pay off a county council and Northern Bank loan for the new house we had moved into during the 1970's, a spacious four-bedroom abode offering this young man a palace to reside in just yards from the old homestead.

This period also coincided with the only occasion in the history of Longford GAA when Rathcline senior footballers won a county championship final, a day when my late brother Pat Mullooly shone brightly on the field at Pearse Park, scoring goals and points at will against Clonguish and launching a successful inter-county career. Longford's 'Bomber', they would later call him.

My days in Lanesborough Vocational School were among the happiest of my youth. For the first time I was under the professional tuition of a teacher with a passion for English. Sheelagh Stafford lived in Ballymahon and only taught in the school two or three days a week, bringing French and English to our timetable, but she was an inspirational educator who believed in making her students live and breathe the subject they were learning. As a result, we were brought to places like the Abbey Theatre to see Stephen Rea in Hamlet and even to Paris itself on a memorable school tour in the early 1980's when we were dragged from our parochial surroundings to speak the language of the French and make sense of the Palace of Versailles. She also brought public-speaking into my life for the first time, prodding and pushing us into public debates organised by the third-world relief agency Concern against other secondary schools. We also treaded the boards in amateur drama productions and concerts, growing in confidence and much, much more. All of a sudden English was no longer a boring subject and I was hooked on both the written and spoken word.

It was during Sheelagh Stafford's reign in Lanesborough Vocational school that I also met with the woman who told me I should try and make a literary career of it all. I really don't know how it came about, but author and novelist Maeve Binchy was in Longford for a one-day workshop at the then St. Oliver Plunkett's Vocational School. I was brought in and settled back among dozens of other students from around the county to listen, but within a short while we were dispersed to write our own short stories and show what we had to offer. I returned some time later with a yarn about a fictional character called Frank Sponato, an Italian spy in the strange world of international espionage. Coming to my seat in the classroom and having read the three or four pages before her, this bestselling author shook my hand saying, "You, Sir, must continue to write," in a tone that left me quite mortified. "You have a great imagination, so make the most of it no matter what you choose to do," she said. I decided to take the advice.

Unfortunately I didn't get the points in my Leaving Cert in 1983 to pursue the course in journalism I wanted at the Rathmines College of Commerce. Ironically, having fared much better in the technical subjects of engineering and maths and, after an hour of career guidance from counsellor Albert Gill on the Rathcline Road, I set off to the Athlone Institute of Technology to do a mechanical and plastic engineering course. As soon as I set foot in the place I knew I had taken the wrong decision and began again to plot a return to the world of journalism and broadcasting.

I owe a debt of gratitude to the Longford Leader reporter Jim Gray for the opportunity to take that route only a few short months later. Back on the news-stands after a prolonged and bitter strike, the Longford Leader provincial paper was led by a new editor Eugene McGee. From darkest North Longford, he was and still is a very straight-talking hack, and while Gray was hospitalised for an illness a junior reporter named Eddie Coffey stepped up to become deputy editor. A vacancy for what McGee would first call 'a general dogsbody' now existed in the newsroom, and when my brother Pat told him of the ambitions of the young man at home, McGee decided to give the apprentice a chance. I began my career in journalism with the highly exotic role of proofreader and copywriter, also typing up statements for the accounts department on quiet days. It was a wickedly entertaining routine. Every day my cousin Joe Mullooly gave me a lift into the Market Square offices of the Longford Leader where I scanned the newsprint for spelling errors and gremlins, and on a Tuesday night I had the added bonus of helping put the paper to bed by attending in the final hours of production. I returned to the office usually after 7 o'clock from Lanesborough on the back of a Honda 90 (donated to me by my brother Donal), sat there for seven or eight hours reading and correcting the proofs and set off for home after it was all over through wind, rain and frost as the seasons turned. For this I was paid the grand sum of thirty two pounds and fifty pence a week by McGee and what was then 'Manpower' before FAS was born. I earned every penny of it, and enjoyed it too.

When I did 'graduate' to covering weekly assignments for the 'Leader' I began to learn from some of the masters. McGee was a superb writer on local issues, with a bluntness for the blatant truth in much of his work. John Donlon was the then 'Longford News' supremo and long before he left for the Star and the Sunday World the proud Moydow man always captured the essence of what Longford people wanted to read about. Paul Williams was also in the News at that time and on Friday afternoons we had the honour of covering Committee of Agriculture meetings together, dealing with sheep scab, TB and headage payments before escaping from the Teagasc centre in the car park in Longford to Andy Byrne's bar nearby for the post match analysis.

My next big break was to be assigned by Eugene McGee to lead the charge across the border into Cavan and to establish a new edition of the paper there. The Longford Leader was already sold every week along the border of the two counties in places like Arva, Gowna and Mullahoran but, with the editor now instilled as manager of the Cavan senior football team, there was an opportunity to grow the brand and extend sales northwards and I was well up for the challenge. The initial foray was hugely successful. We were dispersed into places like Ballyjamesduff, Ballinagh and Cornafean to do features and stories to be printed on pages that would make up a new Cavan edition, and such was the success of the move that McGee finally took the decision to print a separate Cavan Leader title in the late 1980s. These were halycon days for local papers and everyone who worked in the new fledgling publication. We were not so much taking on the great Anglo Celt newspaper that had reigned in Cavan for so long, but chipping away nicely at its derrière. Over a two-year period real progress was made and a vibrant audience was grown, especially in the five large towns of Cavan, Cootehill, Bailieborough, Virginia and Kingscourt. It was also the busiest period of my life: we had a small but very committed team in the Cavan Leader and we worked our asses off to make it work.

With McGee as manager of the football team for a short period, we had also stolen a bit of a march on our opponents. The paper came out a day earlier than the Celt with the Cavan team on the front alongside the insights of the Breffni manager, and we did new features and personality profiles and interviews in a style the people of Cavan had never seen before. We had cartoons, crosswords, spot the ball competitions, sports quizzes and much more. The Celt had been largely full of court-reporting and local authority material, but in the face of a very different alternative they changed their tune over the following few years and became a much better local paper in the eyes of many.

As deputy editor of a small local paper, I was now one of the youngest journalists in the country fulfilling this role. McGee oversaw some of the production but it was my job to commission articles, push out an advertising team, and recruit new local notes correspondents and writers. We employed a few good ones too. Damien O'Reilly (of RTE Radio Countrywide fame) has strong Cavan roots with a passion for Breffni Park and got a start in the Leader, as did Kerryman Gerard Ryle who went on to be deputy editor of the Independent and has since become a very successful investigative journalist in Australia. Paul Healy from Rooskey came in as an enthusiastic soccer writer but emerged as a brilliant journalist, an expert colour writer and a future editor of the Roscommon Champion and Roscommon People. Reporters like Seamus Bradley, Eithne Tynan and Kevin Carney all made their mark to help expand the newspaper, and Sean McMahon from Belturbet was one of our first recruits in the new local notes section, later going on to become a very fine senior journalist in the Anglo Celt.

We had lots of headaches too kick-starting the new production. The paper's layout was half-prepared in Longford forty-five miles away and errors were made. You might call it 'lost in translation' and, when the Editor Eugene McGee went off with the Irish compromise rules football side in Australia, it fell to me to be in court for the settlement of a defamation case. It was a sobering experience for a very young journalist, but, such was the success of the Leader in its infancy, that I buckled down again with our team in Farnham Street and worked even harder to continue the progress. We started to do things the Celt would never do, running promotions like the 'Search for a Star' talent competition through the paper and on stage in local venues. Former Breffni radio legend Phelim Cox acted as MC as hundreds of people who had never bought a Leader turned out and took part. We didn't appreciate it at the time but Phelim was in the same league as Ryan Tubridy (and an awful long way ahead of Simon Cowell) when it came to presenting the talent show and the crowds loved it.

Such was my belief in the future of the Cavan Leader that I finally went to Eugene McGee with Hugh Lynch from the accounts department and a few more colleagues with an offer to buy the newspaper. The office and most of the computers were leased but we had a good team there with Owen Carolan and Ann O'Donoghue in advertising and two smashing staff photographers in my time - Patrick Cummins and Ian McCabe. The readership was good and we felt we could make it even better with a Cavan-based management and by cutting the umbilical cord with Longford. McGee did not accept our initial offer and I got bored with the waiting and walked away to start a new career in broadcasting, but not before building the best relationship of all with a Cavan person, my wife Angela O'Reilly. I met this magnificent Mullahoran woman while she worked in reception in the Leader for a short while, and even though she left to join the Gardai, we stayed together and set off on the next stage of our journey in life. That was probably the best decision I made in all my time in Cavan.

It was during the days of the Cavan Leader that local radio was born in Ireland. I watched with some envy from the wings as station after station popped up around the country, parties were staged to launch new presenters, and there was great excitement as thousands of people got their own locally-based radio service, and legally too. I had been at some of the early events organised by Shannonside Radio in Roscommon and Longford. Mayo man John Morrin was the chief executive and, when he asked Longford-based presenter Niall Delaney to be head of news, there was a really good vibe about the standard of journalism in the station. Delaney was based in Shannonside's offices at New Street in Longford town (opposite the Tally Ho pub, wonder why that sticks in the memory?) and even though I was still working on the paper in Cavan, we sat down and created a Sunday lunchtime current affairs show called 'Primetime' of all things. The idea was to get away from the rip-and-read nature of so many bulletins on local radio. We also tried to get some depth on the critical stories that affected the area in a week and we used to spend most of the day every Saturday plotting a course that usually annoyed somebody in authority.

Our finest hour was definitely a short documentary piece on a pre-election promise that Albert Reynolds, then Minister for Finance, had made in Longford when a helicopter emerged from the sky one day within sight of a general election carrying a Brazillian flax company manager on board who was allegedly going to set up a new plant in Longford and create jobs. With polling day long over and still no sign of the promised jobs, Delaney and I set out to question everyone who had anything to do with that pre-election showbiz style event. There were a real sense that it was a pre-election stunt of the highest category and we interviewed official after official to try and explain what exactly had happened because there was not an iota of a job created at that stage. With no real answers or explanations forthcoming, the final section of the piece could only come from one source, so we tracked down a number for the company itself in Brazil and made a long-distance call seeking answers. We got a manager on the end of a very crackly phone line in Rio de Janeiro and Delaney asked the hard questions. The vagueness of the answers was truly shocking and we knew we had a very decent piece of radio on our hands.

At the edit on the Saturday it fell to me to select an appropriate piece of music to cover the transition from Irish-based story to an interviewee in Brazil and for some strange reason I chose the great Gypsy Kings version of 'Volare', a song recorded by Italian singer-songwriter Domenico Modugno. Written by Franco Migliacci and Domenico Modugno, it was released as a single on the first day of February 1958 and hadn't even a smell of Brazilian origin, but the mention of flying into the clouds and the international feel to it just seemed to fit the mood being created as we headed abroad in search of answers about this Longford flax factory that never was.

The piece was broadcast to some very favourable local reaction and submitted later for the consideration of the judges in that year's AT Cross National Media awards. A few months later Delaney and

I sat at a table with the big nobs of Irish journalism in a top Dublin hotel when it received a national award. The adjudicators were so impressed with the piece they even played it again over the PA system, with howls of laughter when the transition music to Brazil came on again. Afterwards John Morrin, Niall and myself spent hours in the company of Con Houlihan, another award-winner that day. The Evening Press writer was one of my idols in journalism, and here he was telling us yarns about the great Kerry teams of his lifetime in a Dublin pub on a Friday afternoon. It was at this stage it dawned on me that we had made it to the big time at last.

I went full-time as news editor to Shannonside radio after Niall Delaney moved to Sligo in April 1991. It was a brilliant time to take over in the newsroom because Albert Reynolds was now on the way up in the Irish political scene and threatening to unseat Charles Haughey. Week after week Albert was available for interview locally. Practically every Monday he was doing something in the constituency and so the opportunity fell for the local press and media to interview him, but not just on local topics. Soon we found ourselves feeding the dailies with newslines on the economy, Northern Ireland and the currency crisis as it unfolded. Reynolds was not the straightest talker I ever interviewed but he was always available, and some of the national hacks could never understand how we got so much out of all those interviews. As Haughey's calamitous grip on power began to unravel, Albert's tone changed. All of a sudden he was going on the record that he most certainly would be interested in the leadership when Haughey left the stage. There was a very definite twinkle in his eyes and a wink as soon as the tape had stopped rolling. We began to realise the biggest prize of all was heading his way.

The way it happened was extraordinary for both Reynolds and Shannonside radio. RTE's news journalists were on strike when Sean Doherty implicated Haughey in the phone-tapping of journalists while being interviewed on the Nighthawks TV show and within days we were faced with the prospect of having no proper coverage of Albert's rise to the top. So I went to John Morrin and planned the launch of a new programme to capture the election of Reynolds to the highest office in the land. 'Ireland AM' (why didn't we patent these titles?) would be co-presented with yours truly and Gareth O'Connor from Buswells Hotel in Kildare Street, Dublin. (Gareth worked at the time with Northern Sund radio in Monaghan but went on to a successful role in national TV and radio). It was to give Longford its very own ringside seat for the rise of Reynolds to the top table and was an immediate success. In a chapter later in the book I will deal with that famous day when Jim Tunney unveiled the new Fianna Fail leader to us in the Jury's Towers Hotel in Ballsbridge.

From that point onwards we had the number-one politician in Ireland on our show every Monday and Tuesday. The new Taoiseach spoke about Aughnacliffe and Iran, Mostrim and Maastricht, Kenagh and Kuwait and we milked it to the highest degree possible, sending details of the resulting interviews to the daily papers who kindly credited us for most of our work. The tragedy was that Albert only lasted as Taoiseach for less than three years, but by the time it was over I had taken my chances in local radio and had been offered a position on a new RTE television show. Grabbing the opportunity with both hands, I said goodbye to Longford. I was sad to go but the opportunity was too good. Seamus Duke, who expertly produced my 'Mullooly at Midday' show for over a year, was one of those distraught when I announced I was leaving and, true to form, my colleagues and I had one last great blowout at the Park House in Edgeworthstown before I said goodbye. It was time to move on.

'Ear to The Ground' was a really terrific show to work on. John Cummins from Agtel Communications gave me the job after an audition in which I interviewed the Leitrim Fianna Fail TD John Ellis along the street in Drumshanbo, but from the very beginning Mairead McGuinness laid down the law when it came to story research and presentation. The facts had to stand up well behind everything we did: it was either a good story or it was not on air, nothing in between.

We had to find people who were articulate and could hold a good presence on TV and we had to get around every corner of the country. I thoroughly enjoyed the travelling. In those days we spent Mondays in the office in Dublin and left for the country in a jeep full of cameras and technical gear on a Tuesday evening. Driving across Ireland in a big Toyota 4X4, we usually ended up somewhere along the western sea board before nightfall, got a bite to eat and a bed for the night before rising at daylight to set off shooting our first story. For three days we would drive up and down the boreens of Ireland in search of those wonderful characters the show exposed and those thorny issues that were important, working literally from morning till night before returning to our hotel or B & B base. It was hard going but I enjoyed it very much. We also had a very good crew with us. Liam Lavelle and Siobhan O'Gorman cracking the whip as directors and producers, while Mick O'Rourke, Ronan Fox and others were behind the camera. We really had our ear to the ground and it showed on air with good ratings and a second season quickly confirmed. The only problem for me with 'Ear To The Ground' was the short season it was actually on air. After 26 weeks the show was gone for another 5 months and the whole crew was also out of work. My fellow presenter David Kavanagh went home to his farm in Wexford. Yours truly had to return to Longford and start looking for a job fairly sharpish and, even though there were some offers, the quality of the positions available was not hectic.

It was around this time that I managed to get my foot inside the door of the RTE newsroom in Dublin. The then Director of News Joe Mulholland, who created 6.1 TV News, was experimenting with a new feature in the show, a daily slot known in the business as an 'opt out' where the national TV network broke up its transmission footprints and the regional news from your area was presented instead - a bit like the BBC Northern Ireland soccer results used to burst in and spoil the end of BBC Grandstand every Saturday afternoon! I was offered the chance to do the midlands news opt out from the RTE studios at St.

Mary's Square, Athlone, County Westmeath and took it as quickly as I could. A former Marist Brothers school, my new workplace was an austere looking place with a tiny television studio in between several small offices, but the RTE Correspondent Tom Kelly was polite and helpful and quickly showed me the ropes. With cameraman Neilius Dennehy and soundman Norman Dungan I set off around the midlands in search of stories and content for our evening news slot and, when I returned to Athlone, video editor John Joyce beautified it all before it went on air. I had lots of help and solid advice. Former Midlands Correspondent Gerry Reynolds gave me all the encouragement I needed. Studio researcher Anne Brennan ensured we had some sort of a yarn to report on every day and I began to get the hang of the job. There were a few technical teething issues with the transmission of the midlands opt-out news, but within a short few months RTE were advertising again for fulltime journalists in the newsroom in Donnybrook and I immediately put my hat in the ring. It was a permanent position this time so 'Ear To The Ground' was put to one side and the experience of having worked on the opt outs was a great plus. I was offered the job by Joe Mulholland and moved back to Dublin.

I have to say I was sorry to leave 'Ear To The Ground' behind permanently but I quickly got to like the new position on the TV desk in the RTE Newsroom. I was being shown the ropes by skilled professionals like Una O'Hagan, Mary Wilson and young guns like Rachael English and Paul Reynolds were there too. The TV desk is a bit like the fire brigade chasing unit of the newsroom and you can be either very, very busy or redundant for days but I got the hang of it quickly and made some great friends there. When Joe Mulholland advertised the position of midlands correspondent in 1995 I was immediately interested. The bright lights of the city were certainly attractive but I always wanted to come back to my own part of the country. While I enjoyed travelling around the region, I also wanted to be nearer to my elderly parents and my ever-patient girlfriend Angela. I remember the day I emerged from Mulholland's office with the news I had got the job back in the midlands. The big grin on the face obviously gave it away easily. "No need to ask how you got on," said Anne Doyle, the first person I met in the newsroom, "When are you going home?"

For the last 21 years I have been at home at the RTE Midlands studios in Athlone, expertly supported by Paula Murray and Anne Brennan, firstly at the old offices in St. Mary's Square and, since 2014, in a more modern suite of offices at the Athlone Institute of Technology on the East Campus. As a regional correspondent I am part of a team of experienced journalists who bring what goes on outside the pale onto the national TV screens every night and I have been privileged to work closely with some of the finest over the years - none more so than Jim Fahy the doyen of correspondents in the west, now retired in Tuam after a lifetime of distinguished service to RTE.

It has been two very busy decades of life with some incredible highs and lows. The sudden death of my brother Pat from a heart attack in 2000 was a defining moment that has shaped my life and probably scarred it too. The death of my elderly parents brought to an end my link with the house where I was reared in Lanesborough, but my wedding to Angela in 2000 and the subsequent birth of our two glorious young boys have been the factors that has given meaning to everything in the life I live. Without these three people I do not know how I would ever survive, especially returning after a day of torture reporting on tragedy, death and destruction on behalf of RTE News. Such is the life we live. Yet for all of the difficult news stories we cover and the mixed emotions I have to say I still love my job. Seldom can anybody say that every single day of their life presents a fresh challenge and a very new landscape but that is very much the case in my position. There is no groundhog day in our lives, just a different set of people and a very different set of challenges to confront every day we go out to work.

I have on occasion had the opportunity to delve into areas of society where secrecy dominates and very often inequality reigns.

One such was the time spent reporting on the misdiagnosis of breast cancer in nine women who were attending the Midland Regional hospital in Portlaoise in 2008. Each had undergone breast checks and been assured that they were in the clear from cancer, free to get on with their lives. Slowly but surely it emerged that very serious mistakes had been made and for some the new outcome was fatal. Acting on a tip-off from one of those brave ladies I exposed on RTE News the errors that had been made and, after months of analysis and huge political fall-out, the cancer services were discontinued at the hospital. Today many of the women at the centre of my initial reports are no longer with us but these checks are now carried out at a major centre of excellence in a Dublin unit and the women of the midlands are better off for it. Sadly my own sister Nuala died after the discovery of a brain tumor in 2011 - another body blow for my family, the second of my siblings to depart this life. There have been many other such issues and topics I have reported upon, stories that have entertained and intrigued many along the way, tales that have made people laugh and cry, and adventures that have taken me to some of the most difficult places and circumstances. In this book I will be taking a nostalgic look back on many of those episodes in my life in the media, recalling through the archive of over ten years of newspaper columns I wrote in the 'Roscommon Champion' the experiences I had, the highs and the lows and the lessons learned. We will 'flash back' to the original articles written in the Champion and based on my experiences at the time. We will also update some of the stories and examine the changes that have taken place. This is very much a local and a very personal journey for me. I want to reflect on the incredible changes that have taken place in our part of rural Ireland, the very tough challenges that face us all living in the beautiful corner of the isle, and start a real debate on the way we can all work together to restore and renew the countryside we all love so much.

Chapter 1

# DEATH OF A WAY OF LIFE

I grew up in a town that had a love affair with fish. Lanesborough in the 1970s and 1980s was a world-renowned venue for coarse angling. A stretch of the river Shannon where hot water emerged from the ESB power station was the bees' knees for bream, perch and roach, and thousands came to fish here every year. The fish loved the temperatures there and stayed around in great numbers, the fishermen reaped the dividend with bulging nets each day, and the town thrived financially as a direct result. I first began to realise just how lucrative the business was when I started to drink as a young man in the Lough Ree Arms Hotel.

It was never rocket science, just good business. The Lough Ree was expertly run by Margaret Kilroy and her husband Sean, a man who came to town with an All-Ireland football medal with his beloved Offaly in his back pocket. In those days, English anglers came to the hotel in their droves and the Kilroys catered for their every need. The bar in the hotel was on the left-hand side as you came in the door from the main street, and on the right was what was known best as the residents' lounge, the part of the pub where English anglers could sit and drink in peace, watch television, and chat to a few locals. There was a draped curtain on the door with the residents' lounge sign, and all human life was certainly to be found behind it.

The visiting fishermen certainly drank. When the season was in full swing, Sean Kilroy would often proclaim, "A pint, a pike", referring to the rate at which the fishermen would guzzle the stuff after a hard day on their stand at the river. And it certainly seemed that way as dozens of anglers returned to the comfort of the residents' lounge at the end of another sweaty day on the lake and the hotel staff delivered pint after pint of the black stuff before them. In those days, I often sat in that residents' lounge for hours chatting with the fishermen of middle England who came here for the fishing and the craic. Beside me, local character, the great Noelie Gibbons, would engage in conversation with the visitors, teasing out a bit of information on their home towns in Yorkshire, Berkshire or further afield, their favourite sports, their cars and lots, lots more. And they always had hugely interesting stories to tell.

Margaret and Sean Kilroy really went out of their way to make them comfortable and ensure they came back again and again. It was a winning recipe. I remember weeks and weeks in the year when not only was the hotel full, but there were at least another half a dozen houses around the area occupied as the Kilroys called on family and friends to put up visiting anglers for a week. Sterling was flying in and the Lough Ree did well. Lanesborough, Ballyleague, Kilnacarrow, Newtowncashel, Elfeet, Portrunny, Lecarrow and several other local areas benefited hugely from the influx. These were days when the whole culture of fishing was different too, the English angler often arriving with his young son for the week-long stay on the banks of the river, a sight that is almost extinct today.

The people of the town embraced the angling tourism and made as much as they could out of it. Several houses were made available for self-catering and bed-and-breakfast throughout the year. The Anchor Hotel, which was the pioneering forerunner in many respects (before I was even born), and later the Sliabh Ban, played a crucial part. The Baxter, Farrell and Leckey families ran a very professional set up in that hotel and the newly formed Lanesborough Tourism Co-op embarked on a huge modernisation of the facilities for anglers, working with the Central Fisheries board to install concrete fishing stands along the eastern banks of the river. Bernadette Clancy and Des McDermott put hours into attracting the funding and changing the face of the area. Finally the fishermen were being valued a little more by the town, and the business thrived with new competitions and sponsorship coming on board.

The river itself was unfortunately a very different waterway to the stretch that remains today. For starters, I don't recall these new 'islands' in the stretch either side of the bridge in Lanesborough, the chunks of grass, soil and reeds clumped up in their own islands that today practically cut off the fishing areas from the main navigation channel and inevitably led to more weeds and vegetation. In the 80's, from early morning the area would be absolutely 'black' with fishermen perched along the river bank reeling their catches in repeatedly throughout the day. It was the accents that always struck you first whenever you went anywhere near them. A lot of the time as a young lad I hadn't a clue what they were saying, the dialect of the folk from the north of England talking about 'wur nets' and 'wur rods', and the sharp exchanges between friends from down south leaving locals for dead in most conversations.

Where and when it all started to go wrong I'm still not sure. The changes in Sterling are the easiest part to explain. The Irish Pound performed better against its neighbour in the late 1980s, leading to a situation where the English fisherman simply didn't get the same 'bang for his buck'. Later still, inflation was to deliver one of the severest blows. I recall chatting to fishermen on the bridge in Lanesborough who claimed they could now only get a week in Ireland for the same amount of money that paid for two weeks nearly ten years earlier. "We're being priced out of our holiday here," they told me and, when one looked at the soaring costs, maybe they had a point. There is no doubt that

Ireland as a nation priced itself out of a lot of tourism business in that era with high insurance premiums and inflation playing its part. At its most extreme on the east coast, the British tourist was absolutely creased with extra charges for alcohol, food and car hire, but there was a sea-change in the British economy too with not as many families travelling abroad any more. Commercial fisheries began to pop up all over England, offering a new convenient venue for coarse fishing just down the road in places like Yately and Farnborough. I have visited them from time to time and they are hugely popular, not least for the privacy and convenience they give to the British angler, now allowed to sit back ten minutes from home without the cost of a car, a boat trip or a bed in the Lough Ree Arms. It's not hard to see why the trip to Ireland suffered.

As if the economic climate changes were not causing enough problems for our angling tourism, in more recent times the biggest threat of all has emerged on the Shannon banks in the form of an invader with such a notorious international name that it may well soon live up to its reputation as the ultimate 'grim reaper ' and lead to the curtailment of fishing on the famous hot water stretch for the rest of time.

Thursday September 11th, 2014 was the day it all began, and I remember it very well. A few locals trying to improve conditions for fishermen near the bridge had contacted John Devanney and Dr Joe Caffrey, a scientist with the Inland Fisheries Ireland agency. We were all asked to meet at the hot-water stretch in Lanesborough to discuss the growth of heavy weeds there that was choking the fishing in recent times. Joe Caffrey, being as punctual and efficient as ever, was there long before us and when we arrived at the water's edge he had a grimace on his face that I will never forget. "The weeds are the least of the troubles now," he told us, taking a handful of what looked to me like shellfish from the river and pouring them out onto the bank. "Meet the Asian clams."

There was at first a kind of an excited rush of adrenaline about the discovery, an uneducated impression that we were to become the beneficiary of some sort of modern phenomenon that would put our fishery onto a new pedestal. How wrong we were! The fatal attraction of the invasive species, Corbicula Fluminea, to the hot-water stretch at Lanesborough was explained to us all in great detail and, slowly but surely, the most frustrating feeling in the world began to fall upon us, a kind of a depression over anyone who cared about the value of the fishing to the economy here and could remember those glory days of the 1970s and 1980s.

The truth is, the day the Asian clams arrived here was ultimately the day when we confirmed, beyond any reasonable doubt, that coarse fishing at the hot-water stretch in Lanesborough would never be the same again. With its origin in Asia, adult Corbicula are simultaneous hermaphrodites (both male and female) that are capable of both cross and even self fertilization thus taking only one individual to start a population. Adults can live for three or four years, and typically reproduce twice a year, although some populations have been observed reproducing more often under optimal situations. A single adult can produce 1,000-100,000 juveniles per year and that day we were being told that because of the abundance of hot water we had very close to optimal conditions under our nose for our new visitors.

This was devastating news. With the support of a continuous flow of hot water from the power station and the gravel base the clams love, the conditions are absolutely spot-on for reproduction on a mass scale, and that's precisely what had already happened. At the first count the experts estimated that over 30 million of the species were in the stretch, and the implications for the fish are potentially damaging. We know now that Corbicula is a filter-feeder on microscopic plants, animals (including bacteria) and in the water column or in the sediments. The clams live, in other words, on the same sort of feed stuff as our beloved bream and roach and, with their numbers growing thanks to what we have now christened our 'local jacuzzi', we were told that very first day that there is little chance of the fish coming out on top in this particular confrontation.

The most frustrating aspect of the last twelve months has been the lack of progress for all the energy and the effort that has gone into trying to find a scientific solution to dealing with this crippling problem, a campaign that now appears to be ultimately doomed because of the scale of the rolling infestation. Over weeks and months in 2015, local people who cared sat down with fishermen, tourism providers, state agencies and third parties to try and see if they could come up with somewhat of a non-political solution to this most serious threat. I agreed myself to try and help the process during the summer and we sought advice from all corners. There was talk of suction-harvesting, mats on the bed of the river, extractions of all types, redirection of the water outlet from the power station, burning of the shellfish and transport of the critters to approved dumps many miles away, but ultimately no solution that could either guarantee the eradication of the problem or meet the financial constraints set upon those responsible for controlling or removing the Asian clam has yet been found.

Everybody in Lanesborough has slowly come to terms with the fact that the Asian clam is here to stay. The local fishermen had desperately hoped for a management plan that would have the river bed depopulated every two years and a significant investment made in angling locally. One of the central issues that has emerged has been the lack of clarity over who is ultimately responsible for invasive species of this nature in Ireland. While Inland Fisheries led the multi-agency team over the last two years, it seems the National Parks and Wildlife Service have some responsibility in this general area. The sooner it is confirmed who is to lead the campaign to control and manage this very serious problem the better and, even more critically, the issue of providing the funds that the agencies need to really tackle the problem is surely paramount.

Without a more energetic approach from central Government, the problem is getting worse and so too is the threat to fishing Lough Ree, such a short distance away. The clams have already been found, albeit in smaller numbers, at the 'cut' of the shannon navigation into the bay at Ballyleague on the top of the lake. Some of the best fishing experts tell us the very real possibility now exists that one of Ireland's finest predator lakes could well be sterile within 10 to 20 years if the clams spread and unless a more aggressive attitude is taken to deal with the invasive species. We can only hope that the penny will drop with those who can do most. In the meantime, Lanesborough and Ballyleague struggle on in the knowledge that they have been watching this crisis develop, almost in slow motion since September 2014. There's a sense of helplessness emerging, a feeling among many that they have been watching the car career off the road and into the ditch and that now nothing can be done to save the driver. Let's hope they're wrong.

Either way there will never again be a Lough Ree Arms like the one we drank in during the 1980s. Even with the reversal of fortunes for Sterling, it is hard to see the English angler returning in such numbers. Life has moved on, a great tradition is dead, and we are left to pick up the pieces. I salute Hugh Keane, Philip Gordon, Alan Farrell, Gerald Farrell, Eithne Clyne and the members of the Lough Ree Angling hub who have been trying desperately to re-create the atmosphere for angling to grow again here over the last 12 months. The initiatives on the marketing front in the UK and elsewhere have been very praiseworthy and the fishermen have already returned, albeit in smaller numbers. The challenge they face may well be to find a new 'hot water stretch' in the locality where 50-100 stands could well be developed again for coarse angling, hopefully well away from the present invaders and in a corner that will attract both the fish and the fishermen.

Chapter 2

# MEMORIES OF ST MEL'S

Christmas Eve meant only one thing growing up in our house in the 1970's. The ten-mile trip to Longford town had a dual role with two absolutely crucial tasks to be completed once we got there, whether we were driving in hail, wind or snow at that stage. The family's green Volkswagon Beetle would be parked on the back of the Market Square, and my father and I would then be bundled off to St. Mel's Cathedral for pre-Christmas confessions. Meanwhile, my mother would head instead to Vaughan's shop on Ballymahon Street, where her cousin Josie McKenna would have hidden away at least one half tonne of toys for my increased enjoyment that night or during the following day's festivities.

Entering into Josie's home on Christmas Eve was always far more exciting than actually going in the shop. For starters, there were far more toys in the kitchen (and under the stairs and in the hall and upstairs and around the back). Piles and piles of boxes were everywhere and, to a young child of barely nine or ten with a highly creative mind filled with adventure and elf-driven excitement, this was better than any Santa's grotto. This was massive, a major forerunner to anything that Toys-R-Us could ever have dreamed of putting together, with dozens of fascinating and challenging toys and games just waiting to be explored, and a friendly face with a cup of tea for my mother (another Gilleran). Simply put, this was heaven and we all loved it.

The trip to St. Mel's was a different proposition. For starters, it was always described by my parents in fairly clinical terms as 'the Cathedral': nothing more, nothing less. To a young and fairly harmless child from the country, it was a daunting place to visit, a vast open and vacant auditorium with gigantic intimidating columns rising out of sight into the sky on either side and cold marble everywhere else. Warm, it most certainly was not. The atmosphere in the place was also less than memorable at this stage of the day. Long before the midnight mass events would kick off and the crowds would flock here, this was a time when the lights in this great iconic building would be dimmed, practically turned off altogether, and small groups of those seeking redemption would huddle into the seats along the wall on either side of the mega-pillars waiting for their turn to confess, the long periods of silence only punctuated about every eight minutes or so by the abrupt and crushing noise of the sliding confessional grille, moving across and back in one short sharp movement as another happy customer came face to face with the cleric he hoped could save a lost soul in good time for the following day's events.

For the best part of fifteen years, this was how I spent Christmas Eve, the visit to the Cathedral and Josie McKenna's shop religiously observed any time after 3 o clock on the day itself and the job done long before 8 o'clock that night when MIM 302 was turned for home on the Square and faced back for Harbour Row, the metropolis of Killashee and onwards into the sophisticated homeland of George Lane's borough in Rathcline. The country crowd would be home at that stage, the townies left to celebrate the Lord's birth in their own exclusive Cathedral. St. Mary's Church Lanesborough may not have been quite so grand, but it was our chapel and it was home and we were glad to be there.

Since we are now in full confessional mode, this writer must admit he never actually stood in or outside St. Mel's Cathedral at any point on Christmas Day for any of his 45 years until that historic and tragic day in 2009 when watching the place burn alongside hundreds of other deeply shocked and emotional people from the town and surrounds. I woke up that morning in our new home by the Shannon in Ballyleague with a four year old boy in a most excited state of affairs, eyes fixed on a chimney stack and ready to go. With early morning responsibilities related to the man in a red coat with the white beard, I had missed at least five phone calls from the Cathedral Administrator Fr. Tom Healy and a handful of friends around the town. It was only after the last of Bryan Mullooly's small shareholdings in modern Irish toy companies was revealed that my attention got turned to the fire and the destruction that went with it.

My first reaction on hearing about it was one of complete and utter disbelief. Cross-examining a fire-service friend about the scale of the destruction, he kept repeating that even though it was Christmas Day I simply had to come and see it. Only on standing in the car park across the road an hour later and watching the bellows of smoke heading up into the pale Longford skyline, did it fully hit home how really, really bad it was. On the phone Bishop Colm O'Reilly was clearly shaken but polite. He would soon be leaving St. Michael's on the Ballinalee Road to say Mass at the Temperance Hall but, of course, he would come in early and meet me and, of course, he would try and talk about what had happened to RTE News, even if his broken voice revealed just how sad and serious it had now become. At the Cathedral itself there were handfuls of people simply standing around in silence and murmuring among friends about the scale of it all, the damage done so quickly to a building that had taken so long to go up in the first place, and the personal memories they all associated with it.

John McMorrow was my cameraman at the scene, a Leitrim man who had driven from Sligo to capture the historic moment when St. Mel's literally went up in smoke. Circling the building for a better vantage point to reveal the perilous state of the roof, the strikingly scorched cherubs within appeared in his viewfinder through fractured pains of glass as the damage became abundantly clear. The Bishop was quiet-spoken but fiercely emotional and surprisingly determined when our cameras rolled. Yes, the building was woefully wounded after a night when talk of catastrophes during the Midnight mass ceremonies formed such an ironic backdrop. But yes, yes, YES, the cathedral would be re-built, restored and refurbished, of that he had little doubt. With that, he was gone, walking calmly away from the cameras at the gates of next-door St. Mel's College towards the Cathedral smoke and the Temperance Hall with his briefcase in his hand, stopping but occasionally as parishioners wandered over to his side, arms outstretched as if to sympathise with the chief mourner at a terrible funeral.

In the next half hour or so we recorded interviews with some of those who had gathered in complete shock. I remember interviewing three or four people in a row who were simply choking back the tears as they tried to say something meaningful on the day that was in it and others just waved us away. Marian Barnes, for example, talked of the many happy family memories of St. Mel's in its glory, now reduced to smoke and ashes. My English teacher at Lanesborough Vocational School in the 1980s, Marian coached us in the use of English for the exams and devoted many an additional hour on a Saturday to the task. Her tuition was always inspired and her dedication to the teaching of the subject impressive, but today she was in tears and speechless after a while. I was all the more shaken watching it again in the editing process for the RTE evening news. Such emotional interviews brought home that the scenes of devastation and feelings of distress we witnessed that morning were as much to do with the challenge to the faith of the people brought by this inferno as they were a reaction to the loss of a prominent landmark perhaps even more so.

St. Mel's was built originally in the face of adversity, during times when the faith of the Irish people was severely challenged and their very survival put under threat. In the five years after the fire, I watched with great admiration as the plan to rebuild the cathedral was floated and then implemented. Through RTE1's 'Nationwide' programme, I documented the real spirit of the Longford people as they rallied to temporarily turn the sports gym at St. Mel's College into a weekend place of prayer. And eventually I was present at Midnight Mass at the restored Cathedral in 2014 to bear witness to the work which culminated in the Cathedral indeed rising phoenix-like from the ashes.

FOOTNOTE: Josie (Gilleran) McKenna has passed away since the St. Mel's Cathedral fire. We remember her generosity of spirit. I thought about her, my aunt Annie Gilleran and my mother a lot while we were making the TV documentary 'The Longford Phoenix' a few years years later. Josie, Annie and Mollie would have so dearly loved to be there to see the magnificent new building unveiled but more of that later in the book.

Chapter 3

# REELIN' IN THE YEARS

Do you remember where you were the last time recession hit Ireland in the 1980's? It's a question that has been thrown around a fair bit in the last few years as the Irish economy became as sick as a rather large general hospital and some of us with a lot of grey hairs tried to tell a younger generation of how it was somehow much worse back then.

Just out of what was then known as Athlone Regional College when that recession hit, I had got my first job in journalism with the Irish Independent GAA columnist Eugene McGee at the Longford Leader newspaper. While I don't remember too much about the economy in slowdown or recession for the first few years, probably because I was living at home in the safe economy of my mother and father's house, I have clear and lasting memories of the late 1980s when I was sent on assignment to Cavan to set up a new local newspaper there. In retrospect I suppose it was a crazy time to start a new newspaper, but the truth is that we had a fantastic team of young writers and we produced what I consider to have been as good a newspaper as any of the modern day editions around the country. I was proud to be part of that team and still am glad to have my name associated with that paper today.

The Cavan Leader was a tabloid newspaper with a broadsheet agenda. I suppose the only reason we printed in that size was to give people an alternative to the traditional 'Anglo Celt', then one of the country's oldest and most successful provincial newspapers. For the first couple of years we spent most of our time building a readership, and that meant taking on some of the youngest and brightest journalists the county had seen, employing six reporters out of college and other print jobs. We even hired a man in those days who had already worked in TV but that's a story for later in this book. As the economy slowed down and unemployment became one of the big burning issues for our newspaper and its readership, times became much tougher for all of us. My first memory of the 'R' word becoming a weekly feature in the paper's life was the closure of factories in the Cavan area, the long and tedious county council meetings we covered where emigration became a central theme, and the bad debt section of our weekly district courts where much of the time was spent sorting out how much a week some poor individual could afford to pay back to Northern or Ulster Bank for the loan he or she was now being dragged into a court over. Above all, however, I seem to remember that money was simply in short supply, especially in our own newspaper office at No. 21 Farnham Street, Cavan where I can still recall the week to week and day to day battle for a few pounds to get by on.

Believe me, I can honestly say it was a real struggle. By any standards we were poorly paid for starters in the 80's. I'm not saying this to seek anyone's sympathy or anything, because I know most others were in the same boat, but with less than 40 euros of a weekly in salary we struggled to get by. After six months matters improved a little. I became an employee of the paper and, if memory serves me right, my wage was doubled to the princely sum of £70 and we broke out the champagne! By the time we got to setting up the new newspaper in Cavan and recruiting the staff, I was on a few bob more but now, like everybody else, I had to pay for my food and digs and there was the dreaded petrol bill every week. So the expenditure side of the weekly balance sheet was in trouble on a regular basis: cash rich we certainly were not.

Our 'weekly' recession in those days seemed to hit worst on a Wednesday morning. Even though most of us in the newspaper would still have to wait until Thursday evening for the little brown envelope with our wages to appear on the bus from Longford, we were usually stone-broke by ten o'clock on Wednesday morning, and I mean absolutely broke. We simply hadn't a bob between us, not even a pound to put petrol in the car, and that meant the first visit to the day out to the front office to try and break a hole in the petty cash box. 'IOU' notes became legendary throughout that period, not because of the amount of money that was being borrowed for all of 24 hours (because it was all very small stuff), but because of the number of personal notes that would end up in the box and the equally colourful (and non-plausible) explanations that went with them to try and justify the borrowings. Three pounds was as much as some people ever needed, £2 for petrol in the car and a pound to cover a soup and a sandwich that day to tide over to payday on Thursday.

Looking back it was an amazing tale of survival. I don't know did we even realise it was a recession we were living in. I have little or no recollection of that famous Charles J Haughey speech a few years earlier about living beyond our means, and I know that we still had fantastic times. There was great craic between the staff, we had some very late nights out on the back of a fiver, and I made friends in that newspaper that I am still in touch with today. When we look back on it all, we laugh at some of those memories so the times must not have been that bad. Yet the fact remains that it was a recession, people lost their jobs and whole lives were dramatically changed. One wonders how some of the present generation who have never seen such days of poverty will cope with their overbearing repayments in house mortgages and debts in the weeks and months ahead when times get even tougher. These are the young people who got everything without much of a struggle since the 90's, computer games when they wanted them, portable TVs in their bedrooms when they became fashionable, iPods on the very first week when their friends had them and mobile phones for fun. It was a very different age.

I hope I don't sound like a man of a hundred years of age writing about those recessionary days of the 1980s because that was certainly not the intention. What I was trying to simply do was remind some of you that all of this happened before in our own lifetime not so very long ago and the country emerged from it as a better place. The Celtic Tiger brought Ireland back from the brink to become one of the world's greatest economies, mainly because of the young and educated workforce that we had, and hopefully it will do it again in the next decade after the present recession lifts.

*UPDATE: We were not to know it at the time but the local newspaper business was to become the first big winner of the Celtic Tiger era, only then to leave a whole series of new owners with an Armageddon when it all turned to dust as the bubble burst. I left the Cavan Leader in 1991 to work for Shannonside radio news as the recession came to a slow end. Eugene McGee eventually sold the paper to the former Irish army officer Captain James Kelly, a prominent figure in the 1970's Arms Trial controversy and native of Bailieborough, who continued to publish it for a short while. McGee continued to edit and manage the Longford Leader throughout the recession and brought it through to the new millennium when the tide turned in his favour before eventually selling the title to the Scotttish Radio Holdings/Johnson Press Group in 2005 for an estimated £5.8 million. The deal was an absolute disaster for the new UK owners . With the downturn, local paper advertising and sales plummeted and they lost their shirt. In April 2014, the Johnston Press media group sold*

the Leader again and thirteen more regional newspaper titles to Iconic
Newspapers Limited, a company run by British advertising executive
Malcolm Denmark. It's believed the titles were sold for in the region of
€8.5m, not far from the price of the Leader alone in the original sale. The
Anglo Celt was also sold in 2004 for an estimated price of €15 million,
the O'Hanlon family in Cavan ending a tradition of local ownership
for many decades by handing over to Dunfermline Press and the Celtic
Media Group. James Kelly finally closed The Cavan Leader, but during
the boom The Cavan Voice was one of several new titles published around
the country by a group of businessmen which included Niall Mellon - the
charity fundraiser that sent builders to South Africa. Regrettably, it also
suffered when boom turned to bust in 2008 and closed later with the loss
of dozens of jobs. Manpower subsequently became FAS in the years that
followed my days at 21 Farnham Street, offering job subsidies in many
industries and handing on responsibility to other agencies for job creation
in the new millennium.

# Chapter 4

# SAY HELLO, WAVE GOODBYE

In 2004 I bought a cruiser for the Shannon and thus began an adventure that was to bring us as a family all over Ireland in a journey that mixed the best scenery on our shores with meeting some of the most memorable of characters. I have never regretted the decision, for that trusty boat has taken on all sorts of conditions and terrains and come out the other side, even while we as a family have thoroughly enjoyed a different perspective on so many places around the country at a different rhythm of life.

I wrote in some detail at that time for the Roscommon Champion about a trip from County Roscommon to Killaloe, County Clare and the southern end of Britain and Ireland's longest river. The journey on a 1969 steel-hull Dutch cruiser took nearly a week to complete and included a scary account of how at one point Lough Derg's powerful waves threatened to overturn the vessel at the height of the great Irish (windy) summer. No change there obviously.

Several threats were made after that voyage to travel in the opposite direction to the top of the Shannon at some stage in the future and sail into the Ballinamore-Ballyconnell Canal, re-opened to boaters in 1994 and restoring a 38 mile long navigable link between the Shannon and the Erne. In the summer of 2009, despite a few gremlins along the way, we managed to get the boat from Hanley's Marina in Ballyleague to a safe and secure spot north of Carrick-on-Shannon. The man at the lock near Leitrim village made no secret of the vast amounts of energy required for the mission ahead, the restored canal with 16 locks and 31 bridges not being for the faint-hearted. The waterway has three natural sections: a still-water canal with 8 demanding locks (murder!) from the Shannon at Leitrim to Kilclare, a summit level which includes Lough Scur, and a river navigation from Castlefore near Keshcarrigan through Ballinamore and Ballyconnell to the Erne, which has another 8 locks. Marvellous.

Even though all of the locks are now all automated and operated independently, it is still a daunting challenge to get through them for somebody like myself with very limited boating experience. The main issue is the astonishing difference in the levels of the water in the canal as one goes from lock to lock. The canal rises about 80 feet through 8 locks from the Shannon to Lough Scur. From there, passing 8 loughs through the towns of Ballinamore and Ballyconnell, it falls about another 70 feet. Over half the navigation course lies within Leitrim, one-fifth in Cavan, and a short length is to be found on the boundary between these two counties. What's left is on the boundary between Cavan and Fermanagh except for three short stretches of artificial channel totalling about a mile constructed entirely within Fermanagh. It really is a major cross-border project if ever there was one, and sometimes you have to wonder if the money was really spent wisely.

Starting at Lock 16 near Leitrim village was a novel experience. Operating the gate could not be done by a lone boatman, so before the lock I left my brother-in-law to skipper the cruiser while I headed to the river bank with a special card. We had luck on our side as somebody had just come down the canal and the gate was wide open, meaning that our cruiser could go straight in and I could get on with the business of closing the gates with the hydraulic pumps and raising the water level. It was a short-cut we were going to enjoy at the start of this mammoth trip north.

The general agreement was that I had got the handy job: with the lock gates closed on either side, all I had to do was push a button from the top of the lock that sent in dozens of gallons of water from the canal, violently shaking the boat repeatedly back and forth inside the lock and giving the skipper a slightly uneasy time as he tried to ensure the vessel did not go either back too far and hit the closed gate behind or go up too far to the front where it could have had a similar confrontation with the gate there. The process of actually filling the lock with water was a surprisingly quick one. I was accustomed to a much slower time in advancing through river Shannon locks in places such as Athlone and Tarmonbarry, but these were gigantic devices compared to the canal locks so I suppose I should not have been too surprised.

Once the water level had reached that of the canal, another automated switch opened the gate on the north side easily and we proceeded quickly on our journey to the next lock. In the course of just an hour we made our way through another five of these, the only difference being the huge depth of some we passed through. One would not have wanted to be claustrophobic on a job like this as the boat was often stuck at the heart of a lock, a good 20-30 feet below land level and, when water started flowing in, it could really make for a very unsettling experience until you grew accustomed to the sensation. Somebody once compared it to the water breaking into a bog hole while deep down in the peat you were trying to cut some of the last remaining stone turf. I actually thought it was worse than that: getting out of the bog hole would be difficult but possible, yet escaping these giant locks would surely be a different matter and one I wasn't hanging around to test.

In between locks was some of the calmest Leitrim countryside one could ever come across. From here to Keshcarrigan there were a handful of lonely-looking cottages and farm yards along the canal but very little activity to be seen, and we enjoyed the voyage for miles without the interference of man or machine. With poor land on either side of the waterway you could easily see the economic argument for restoring the canal and providing some sort of tourism revenue in these parts. South Leitrim and the western part of Cavan, the regions benefiting from the canal project, are probably the most disadvantaged in the entire country. We always slag off the Leitrim folk for the deprived nature of their county, especially when it comes to football, but the statistics are devastating. In the sixty years from 1926 to 1986, Leitrim and Cavan lost 50% and 35% of their total populations respectively. This is tumble-weed territory, and a look around the barren landscape confirms everything the statistics point to. The wipe-out of all employment in this area was rapid in the years leading up to the campaign for the restoration of the canal. Employment in Leitrim fell by 14% in the 20 years between 1961 and 1981, and by 12% in Cavan over the same period. Between 1961 and 1981, the population of Ballinamore alone declined by 17.5% while in Ballyconnell the corresponding figure was 14%. Emigration is really only a symptom of the lack of employment but it gives us an indication of what happened to all human life in these areas during what were undoubtedly very barren years.

Ballinamore is today one of the more vibrant towns along the canal. Many hours after we commenced our journey and made our way through the beautiful surroundings of Lough Scur, we arrived at the marina there. After cruising past its golf course and under a bridge with the largest tricolour I had seen for a while, we moored and walked through a bustling town in search of refreshments. It was here in 1988 that the International Fund for Ireland financed a detailed feasibility study into restoring the canal. In June 1989, Taoiseach Charles Haughey announced that the two governments had decided to adopt the proposal as a flagship North-South project. After the

World Cup, work commenced on the restoration in November 1990 and it was opened to traffic on time and within budget of £30 million in May 1994.

This was a lot of money to commit to just one project in those days, but such was the scale of the redevelopment work and the machinery and manpower required, every penny was really needed for essentially a new navigation along the line of the original waterway which had never been properly completed in the first place. From Ballinamore to Haughton's Shore and Lough Garadice, we came across some of the most breathtaking scenery of the entire voyage, but closer to Ballyconnell it was back into the Woodford canal section and a timely reminder of the Celtic Tiger era. Around a bend appeared acres and acres of trees in a forest with 30 brand-new log cabins built in its midst. An idyllic setting for a holiday home but, even from the boat, I wondered how well this development was selling and the sight of a half-fitted marina dug out on the land adjacent to the cabins was a sharp reminder of the downturn in the construction business.

If we thought the sight of empty log cabins at this junction in the Cavan countryside had been a bit sad, we certainly were not prepared for what met us as we cruised into the town of Ballyconnell 20 minutes later, dozens and dozens of empty apartments on either side of the river in a relatively small country town and an eerie sight for all to see. Desolate and downtrodden were the words that came to mind, a truly shocking sight. We stayed in Ballyconnell for several days while the rain came down in buckets adding to the depression of the place and eventually forcing us to abandon the onward trip for a few weeks. Each time we returned to check the boat's safety we spotted another empty home along the river and wondered to ourselves again and again, "How the hell did it really come to this? Who planned these developments? Who did they really believe was going to live in them?"

Chapter 5

# THE DAY THE MUSIC DIED

Have you ever worried about the world our sons and daughters will inherit after the present so-called downturn in the global economy has finished or when the International credit crisis that is destablising the financial sector in the United States and around the world comes to an end? Have you ever woken up in the morning and looked at the television pictures of another bank going bust or a company folding and wondered what will be left by the time your beloved son or daughter makes it to the big wide world after school or college? It's sobering stuff.

On Monday morning of this week the latest earth tremors began on both sides of the Atlantic after the collapse of a bank called Lehman Brothers in the United States. We were told pretty sharply that thousands of jobs were at risk after the firm's UK business was placed into administration as a result of the move. Workers arriving at Canary Wharf in London's Docklands financial district described the mood among employees as sombre and even though they said they had been told to turn up as usual they had no idea what was likely to happen. They didn't know it but this was the beginning of the end. The news about Lehman sparked panic in the world's stock markets with big falls in Asia and in the UK, where the FTSE opened more than 100 points down. As I write this, all the world's major financial regulators are on alert, with the Bank of England saying it will be monitoring the fallout and is ready to intervene if it causes fresh chaos in the money markets. The European Central Bank also says it's watching carefully and all because Lehman, America's fourth biggest investment bank, is to file a petition under Chapter 11 of the US Bankruptcy Code. This piece of machinery usually allows companies to reorganise their contractual and debt obligations under the supervision of a bankruptcy court but there had been a series of unsuccessful last-minute meetings in New York to try and save the 150-year-old institution and two potential buyers pulled out of a rescue deal, leading to these TV scenes of panic.

After all the recent 'dig-out' business transactions with the US home lenders Freddy Mae and Fanny Mac, it was deemed inevitable that the bank would turn towards good old Uncle Sam to see if the US state could rescue it but the George W Bush administration refused to bail out the stricken firm with taxpayers' money and so the rest of the world woke up to see pictures of Lehmans' staff leaving the bank in the US in their droves with cardboard boxes under their arms. Very encouraging and heartening scenes, as I am sure you will agree. They tell us that Lehman has been badly hit by the collapse of America's sub-prime mortgage market and the credit crunch. Last week it revealed massive losses of around €3.2bn ($3.9bn) in the last quarter and announced it was cutting 1,500 jobs. Some argue we should have seen it coming. The former head of the US Federal Reserve, Alan Greenspan, has predicted the failure of more major US finance groups. He said the crisis on Wall Street was the worst he had seen in his career and the chances of escaping a recession "less than 50%". So what will remain when all of this is over and how long will it take for the world markets to bounce back? Or will they recover at all?

I suppose I should admit that I might be a tad premature in worrying about the timing of it all and its effect on the next generation in my house. Our first born son is now just three years old. His world at the moment is an absolutely beautiful place, a land where Fireman Sam extinguishes every single blaze in the town day after day without ever losing a life in a fire, Noddy's car seems to run without any petrol, dear or otherwise, and there has never been a run on the Toy

Town bank that we have been made aware of anyway! But, on a more serious note, it's the future we are moulding for the next generation that concerns me and thousands of other parents, the question being what sort of country we will be left with after all this talk of recession and doom and gloom is over, and the direct implications that the present crisis will have on the lifestyle and the character of the next generation.

Let me give a clear and concise example of what I mean. My parents grew up at a time of a mini-industrial revolution in Ireland. The arrival of rural electricity opened new doors for their world, bringing strength and stability to their enterprises and leaving them the opportunity to work hard and earn a living. I like to think they were a confident and an optimistic people as a result of that but emigration took its toll on their world. Their brothers and sisters had to go to England and America to work and only those who could live on the farm stayed behind in the 1950s and the 1960s. I grew up in the 1970s and the 1980s and another world 'global-oil-crisis' of a sort meant several members of our family also had to emigrate, forced to do so by the plight of unemployment and recession. People like the economist David McWilliams have argued that it wasn't until the late 1990's that this nation actually began to recover from the scourge of emigration, a time when our confidence in a new generation of well-educated Irish coincided with our triumph on the world soccer stage and made for a very decent legacy for the next generation. Jack Charlton may never have realised just how important his march into the World Cup in Italy and USA actually was.

In my opinion that 1990s legacy was essentially about giving our sons and daughters the confidence and the optimism that their parents never really had until late in life. And we all know the real value of confidence, what it does for the economy and the state and how it really helps to build a nation. Ask your bank manager the next time you're in his company if you don't believe me. Ask him how important confidence is to the world of finance, especially when he sits down to consider forking you out a loan. And that's at the heart of what I am writing about this week. I have real and genuine fears that the next generation of Irish people will struggle on two fronts because of what has happened, not only in the last ten months but in in the last ten years. Add to that the severity of the most recent downturn and the fact that confidence in any enterprise going forward will be poor, especially in the bank when you go in for a loan, and you begin to see the scale of the challenge facing the next generation.

I believe that my son and thousands like him will have to grow up with a different level of confidence in their veins - a different type of belief in their hearts and a very different type of know-how in their heads. To me this will be essential in their education and formative years because if they don't get this type of training or assistance they may very well struggle in the strange new world that finally emerges after the one where global downturns and international credit issues prevail. And the other worst part about all of this? The self-centred and selfish part. The way things are going on the world markets these young people will also have to start saving to look after their parents in later life. The downturn in the markets has meant that thousands of Irish people facing retirement in the next twenty or thirty years have already lost thousands and thousands of Euro from their pension schemes, and guess who will be asked to help them out and get them into a nursing home when they can no long look after themselves in years to come? Like I said at the beginning, sobering stuff.

*UPDATE: When I wrote this piece seven years ago, I really had no idea the demise of a global financial services firm whose founder was a Jewish cattle merchant was going to have such a devastating effect on the Irish economy and ultimately lead to a bailout by the IMF and the EU that would launch a prolonged recession for Ireland. There was, of course, a huge postmortem on what went wrong in the firm, with a court-appointed examiner saying Lehman executives regularly used 'cosmetic' accounting gimmicks at the end of each quarter to make its finances appear very different and certainly less shaky than they really were. Within days it became clear others were doing the same. AIG, Citigroup and Countrywide also admitted that they were in much worse shape than they initially allowed. The problem for us was the very issue I wrote about in September 2008, the complete loss of confidence here as world markets began to wobble. Our property bubble burst in a most spectacular fashion within weeks. Almost overnight, prices of homes and major projects began to plummet, eventually losing between 60-80% of their value, with huge implications for the banks. Even though we had been assured our financial institutions were all well-funded and had reserves, the Irish banks were hopelessly insolvent, the budget deficit soared to unimaginable heights, and unemployment tripled. The fall in output was probably the largest ever experienced by an industrial country since the Second World War.*

*Ireland quickly found itself unable to borrow on international markets and, in November 2010, had to follow Greece and seek ignominious recourse to an emergency bail out from the IMF and the EU. It was a tough pill to swallow but without it God knows where we would have been.*

*The knock on effect for us all, especially in rural areas of Ireland, has been catastrophic. The words 'ghost estates' entered our lives shortly afterwards as banks cut off the supply and developers folded, leaving hundreds of largely unfinished developments all over our country and especially here in Roscommon and Longford. I spent much of my time in 2012 and 2013 watching the first of these developments being demolished, the hopes of a nation also crumbling as the blocks and mortar came down in places like Gleann Riada outside Longford town. All the time we asked ourselves who did we really think was going to live in all of these empty homes and maybe wondered why the banks had not probed the same issue with a little more tenacity when the developers arrived to seek loans to build them in the first place? The penalties for individuals and families have been appalling. If* you didn't lose your job already in the recession then you got saddled with new charges such as the USC , the 2nd home tax, the property tax, water charges etc and, with incomes diving all the time, families have had to endure huge personal sacrifices and pain. Tragically, suicide was the only option seen by some in our society. I have reported on inquests throughout the last five years when harrowing details of loved ones taking their own lives after years of trying to cope with crippling debt have been outlined. It is soul destroying. On November 29, 2010, the government negotiated a financial assistance package with the EU and the IMF totalling €85 billion (including a contribution of €17.5 billion from Ireland's own resources). The new tightrope was put up and we have had to walk it ever since.

As I write this update there are signs that the recession is indeed coming to an end in cities and large towns along the east coast of our country but precious little is to be seen anywhere else that would lead anybody who is really honest to believe that the big R is no longer a factor in rural Ireland. So the truth is that I worry just as much if not more today about the future of our ten year old boy Bryan as I did in 2008. I really wonder whether the economy of this country will ever return to a state whereby the vast majority of our children can choose to stay here and start their own families. Selfishly, I don't want to see him emigrate when the time comes. I want to see my grandchildren live on Irish soil and I refuse to apologise to anyone for that. There have been some positive developments. Unemployment has fallen but a simple drive through any village or small town in our area in the middle of the day will give you just one lasting impression, stony silence. The small shops are shut, the pubs are closed and nobody is about. Living beside the river Shannon and a terrific water sports facility in Ballyleague the silence factor is even more noticeable. I remember in the days of the Celtic Tiger trying to drive through a car park by the river that was packed with 4X4s and pick-ups, the owners out on the waterways on their jet skis, speedboats and more. Nowadays the same waterway is practically deserted even on sunny evenings and at weekends. There is most definitely a lost generation, a group of local people between the age of 18 and 28 who have left our shores and may well never return.

Chapter 6

# HERE IS THE NEWS

When you turn on the television on a Sunday night at nine o clock and are faced with the sight of the country's Minister for Finance unveiling a dramatic plan to recapitalise the nation's banks to the tune of some €10 billion, you surely realise that we are living in very perilous financial times. The economics experts will tell us that, even though it was all very dramatic, what happened at the weekend was certainly to be expected since Irish bank shares were hammered by investors speculating on exactly this occurring. Worst affected has been Anglo Irish Bank, with its shares dramatically collapsed from a high of €17.50 to 38c when the markets closed on Friday last. In the light of this wipe-out and big falls of other financial stocks, something had to happen. For the banks involved, It's now all a bit like deciding which pension scheme you have to sign up to. Sunday night's decision means banks will have to decide if they actually want to be recapitalised. They will have to submit proposals in January and the government will then be able to take preference shares in return for investment. Those shares have priority over ordinary shares in the payments of dividends and give a fixed return annually, so I suppose some of our hard earned cash will come back if the financial markets ever return to something akin to normality. Other investors will be able to put in money on the same terms if they have the cash, not to mention the confidence in the said banks, and I wonder how many will actually have that? Now that the ball has landed in the banks' court, and based on some of the pronouncements from their CEOs and chairmen in the last few weeks, it's not at all clear that they will line-up immediately to take the cash. I was fascinated on Sunday night by the Fine Gael deputy leader, Richard Bruton, who described the Government's announcement as an attempt to buy time. He told RTE's The Week in Politics programme that it was a preemptive strike rather than a well thought-out strategy, and said that it leaves several questions unanswered. The other opposition parties were not really impressed either. Labour's Finance spokesperson, Joan Burton, said recapitalisation was essential to get money flowing again, but she expressed some doubts that this announcement will achieve that. She criticised the Government for not 'reforming' the banks in the aftermath of the original €400 billion guarantee it provided to them last September. However, both Richard Bruton and Joan Burton said that their parties would not oppose the necessary legislation required to allow the movement of money from the National Pension Reserve Fund to the banks. It seems the only thing that may now slow down the recapitalisation train in the next few weeks may well be the push to bring real change at the banks in terms of the arrival of new faces at management level and the exit of others from the same multi-million euro salary scales. On Monday morning the markets gave their thumbs up to the proposals when shares in the banks listed on the Irish Stock Exchange jumped. AIB shares were 8% higher before lunchtime and Irish Life and Permanent were 6% better off within hours. Troubled Anglo Irish Bank shares added 24% to their value and Bank of Ireland shares rose by 23% within the first half hour of trade, but the silence from the boards of these banks and their corporate headquarters was deafening throughout the day on Monday. I waited with interest to see how the big guns would react when they finally found the courage and the craft to give their reaction to Brian Lenihan's proposals. Throughout Monday morning we waited patiently to see their statement, and waited and waited, but nothing came. It wasn't for the lack of trying to get a response from the bank chiefs. All of the media organisations were quoting the 'no comment' situations throughout the day on Monday .A spokesperson for AIB told RTE that the bank's board would discuss the Government announcement when it meets later this week. The bank said it would discuss the detail and make further comment then, but not until the board has had an opportunity to meet. Bank of Ireland said they had no comment overnight and Anglo Irish Bank also said that they had no comment other than stating rather blandly to the newspapers that they were "noting the Government's statement". The media also reported on Monday that Irish Life and Permanent had no comment to make either and EBS said it was not going to say anything. Like many others I found all of this deeply disconcerting. It wasn't as if the banks were not expecting the announcement from the Government in the last few weeks, and some of us were foolish enough to believe that once the deal was put on the table their boards of directors would have been hobnailing it into emergency meetings on Sunday night or Monday morning all over our capital city to try and do the number-crunching within hours. By two o clock on Monday there was still not a smidgen of a comment from the banks. The closest we got was a statement from the union representing bank workers who gave a cautious welcome to the deal on the table, but the IBOA General Secretary, Larry Broderick, was still saying that the union was still concerned that the Minister for Finance has not yet ruled out the possibility of private equity funds being involved in the future of Irish banking. The IBOA warned that they would be engaging further with the Department of Finance, the regulatory authorities and the senior management of the financial institutions over the coming days in order to ensure that staff concerns are taken into account, and gave a clear warning that they feared the arrival of private money or state cash in the banks might mean a fairly tight look at staffing numbers and issues like that, issues which they have been very quick to point out should not be on the table at all at times like this. The problem for the Government is that the ordinary taxpayer will expect them to do just the opposite in the coming days and take a very economical look at each bank, its staff numbers and the performance of its CEOs.  We know now the most senior executives at Irish banks earned close to €100 million in the last four years, despite serious misjudgments over the property market that led to the Government having to bail out the entire banking system last October. To the layperson, the scale of salary levels for these chief executives are shocking. Bank of Ireland boss Brian Goggin has made almost €23.5 million since landing in the bank hot seat four years ago, with pay packages alone coming to about €11.4 million. Since he took the helm in 2005, the remuneration package of Anglo Irish boss, David Drumm, is worth over €21 million, including pay packages totaling almost €9 million. Drumm's right hand man Willie McAteer was awarded remuneration of over €18.6 million in the last three years and, even though profits at AIB have tumbled, their chief executive Eugene Sheehy's remuneration could top €11.4 million since taking the top job in 2005. Not to be outdone, Irish Life & Permanent also saw profits tumble 88% as mortgage lending dried up this year, yet chief executive Denis Casey, who sold half of his shares in the group last year, could earn up to €3.35 million since taking over the top job in May 2007.  Watching all of these big pay-outs in the wings is the ordinary taxpayer like you and me who will certainly expect Brian Lenihan to come forward with a major shake-up at management levels if all of these banks are to avail of our national pension funds early in the new year. Or is it the case that the top men in the banks think they can survive it all? Will they brazen it out? Or have they finally realised that with accepting these huge salary levels comes the responsibility to ensure that the share price stays in good shape. Watch this space.

Chapter 7

# WHEN THE PARTY STOPS

It's seven o clock on a Saturday evening in Salthill near Galway city centre and at least a hundred people are queuing outside a pub. Now when was the last time you saw anything like that? Either side of the doorways of this impressive bar two bouncers slowly and methodically allow the patrons into the premises and, one by one, they disappear from the busy street to get on with their Saturday night entertainment only for another group of enthusiastic drinkers to take their place in the queue. At ten past seven the crowd is still thronging the footpath outside the bar and I've seen enough to make me wonder what exactly is going on, so I wander over a bit closer to the premises as my nose gets the better of me. I make a few discreet inquiries.

Over the door the name of this particularly popular licensed premises stands out in big capital letters. KRCMA, apparently pronounced Krutch Ma, opened it's doors in 2005. To solve the mystery of the crowds I seek guidance and am told the name translates to the English language as 'pub' . Better still it's what's known in the new modern multicultural Ireland as a Slavic pub! I don't know about you but I have never been in a Slavic pub before but I notice that almost all of the people in the queue are male, almost every single one, and there seem to be an awful lot of Polish men there too. It's not just a pub either. The owners are Slovakian and the food menu is mainly eastern European. I am reliably told that KRCMA has carved out a successful niche for itself attracting not only foreigners living in Galway but also curious locals who have grown to like the place. It still bills itself as a bar and restaurant but the pub itself is a substantial size with multiple levels. Those of you who frequent Galway city or have gone to college there will remember some of the previous pubs that have operated in the same corner of Salthill such as Scruffy Duffy's. Inside the bar is spacious and well designed. There are two pool tables which are becoming more of a rarity these days in any pub around the country and I am told by locals that large gigs such as reggae and house music nights often take place there. The size means they can easily accommodate large crowds and by the look of things this evening the Eastern Europeans are reacting very positively to this new business venture.

The party I am with have booked a restaurant table at a popular Italian place next door so we adjourn there to enjoy the rest of the evening. Some time after nine o clock we re-emerge onto the wet streets of Galway and look around at a very lonely and vacant promenade but the situation hasn't changed much at KRCMA. Outside the pub is a nice patio area with a large canopy ideal for outdoor smoking and drinking and now the crowd numbers have swelled again. The pub obviously abides by the same smoking laws as every other pub in the country but instead of just a trickle of smokers outside there are at least thirty men in under the canopy. Behind them the bar seems to be full again to overflow and as I drive away from the area I find it all bemusing and ever so slightly curious.

On Sunday the scene of a long queue outside a pub at seven o clock in the evening is still on my mind, so I take the opportunity to ring a colleague from the media who lives in Galway and ask him about it all. "It's what you might call a 'Paddy Flahertys' for the Polish and the eastern Europeans" he tells me. "We've all seen enough Irish pubs abroad when we go away and work in other parts of the world, well this is the Slavic equivalent here in Ireland!" My friend tells me that the bar does an outstanding trade all week but particularly at the weekends when it appears that the Polish travel from all over the country to be with their friends in Galway and enjoy a drink or a meal. "It's always jam-packed when I pass it," he says. "Mind you, we have not seen much sign of the recession affecting queues for anything in this city at the moment." After a week when the nation learned officially for the first time that we are in a recession I find the scenes I witnessed in Galway last weekend to be highly ironic and, in some ways, deeply concerning. Anybody who has ever had to say goodbye to a member of their own family in Shannon airport en route to America to start a new life will not begrudge the eastern Europeans their opportunity to come to Ireland and make a living here. The problem is that after all the doom and gloom of the last couple of months one must wonder what is to come of the patrons of KRCMA bar in Salthill over the next couple of years as our economy slowly but surely downsizes into what it once used to be. Where will the jobs come from for these people? How will they provide for their families here? And, more importantly, if they are forced to leave these shores because of a lack of employment, where will they go? The economic experts tell us that, despite huge growth in recent years, returning home will not be an option for a significant percentage of these people. The Economist newspaper reported recently that eastern Europeans are facing their own mini-recession. Wage costs are creeping up. Labour shortages are biting. Out-of-date infrastructure, such as Poland's notorious roads, are clogging trade and in several countries inflation is rising. Home ain't going to be sweet for most of them.

The weaknesses in infrastructure in Slovakia are there for all to see. This time last year I was one of a group of people who stayed in Bratislava for a few days while supporting the Republic of Ireland soccer side. To say I was stunned by the poverty outside the city centre would be putting it mildly. The sight of a battered old red tram pulling up at hovels only two or three miles from the capital city and letting off the down and out after a days begging was enough to confirm that the Slovaks have their own problems to solve. The old battered tram was a real flashback to the old Soviet Union for me and it is hard to see how any of their emigrants here will be able to go back and get fulfilment there if the Irish bubble bursts for them.

The reality is that the so-called global recession holds out as much danger for the people who drink in the KRCMA bar in Salthill as it holds for us the native residents of Ireland. Amidst the depression of last week's economic reports on TV and radio there was an admission that the problems being experienced in the US and the UK are so serious that they could destabilise several other economies around the world and that scenario has to be a deeply concerning one for us all. How the present problems will be overcome remains to be seen. While George W. Bush puts his faith in bailing out the banks and the markets in the United States this week the British government continues its new policy of nationalising the financial institutions and all the time we wonder when will the Irish banks start to lose their nerve in the face of such international instability?

"Every generation looks after its own" - a wise old commentator told me last week after I first raised the issue of how the present difficulties will shape the economy for the next generation. But one really has to wonder how it will all pan out down the line after all of this financial turmoil, how it will affect natives and migrants here and if we will ever again see Slovaks queuing in such huge numbers to get into a pub in Salthill at seven o clock on a Saturday evening.

*UPDATE: It is estimated that over a hundred thousand Polish people live in Ireland but it was a newspaper article on just one of them, a woman called Magda (not her real name) published in in 2012 that cast the issue of social welfare support for non-natives into the national limelight with contrasting reactions.*

*'Magda' had apparently given a frank interview to a leading Polish newspaper in which she spoke about living in Ireland and what it was like for her. The paper was doing a feature on Poles living here and how they were doing in the recession and Magda talked about our generous welfare system and how it enabled her to have a wonderful life here without working. She talked about walking the beach in the early morning and being free of the stress that comes with a job. The article had been lifted for use by an*

*Irish newspaper but unfortunately some of the details seemed to get lost in translation. It was suggested Magda was living a high life here with the financial supports but didn't really think much of what Donegal had to offer. In fact the woman didn't say either of these things. What she actually said was that she had done a course in Hawaiian massage while here, and that although she thought Donegal was the most beautiful place in the world, others (presumably locals who can't get a job and are being forced to emigrate) think it is a s\*\*\*hole.*

*For a few days a debate raged about the "foreigners coming to our land and taking our social welfare cheques." The usual suspects in Irish life joined in and lamented the soft attitude towards the Polish, and we began to get a view of how life in this recession might not be so attractive for the Eastern Europeans, accused by extremists as being welfare tourists on our soil. Fortunately the properly translated version of Magda's story was published within a few days and most commonsense folk began to see the difficult nature of the life she was living in the remote North West. It turned out this young woman was not reeling in the cash and living the high life after all but was just about getting by on €188 per week and really wanted to get a job but was unable to do so.*

*The truth is that from 2012 onwards people like Magda have left our shores in their thousands. Research shows a 15% rise in the number of foreign nationals looking to move from Ireland to Australia, Canada and New Zealand up to 2014. People from countries such as Poland, Lithuania and Romania were top of the list seeking a way out and that includes hundreds of skilled people who have worked here over a number of years but are struggling because of high unemployment. Rather than stay, or else return to their own home countries, many were looking to move to faster-growing economies outside Europe, alongside tens of thousands of Irish nationals on the same planes. Fluency in the English language was the dividend this country gave them, boosting their chances in their new destination countries with a language. In 2013 over 50,000 non-Irish people had emigrated from this land, following 41,000 who had left in 2012.*

*KRCMA is still open at Upper Salthill, Galway.*

Chapter 8

# POSTCARD FROM AMERICA

The atmosphere in the shops along New York's 5th Avenue was distinctively strange this week. At the Rockefeller plaza in the heart of the 'Big Apple' the skating rink was still covered with enthusiastic young Americans enjoying their day out on the ice, but in many parts of the city of New York there were also a coolness in the air with signs posted in the front windows of many shops that I have never seen before in these parts.

'Going Out Of Business' was the one that caught my attention more times than any other. In side-streets, along avenues all over the city, and uptown in the Irish suburbs I saw that sign time and time again as shoppers gathered to take advantage of the concluding days of businesses trading. Lots of different types of enterprises seem to have been already badly hit here by the housing market crash and the economic crisis on Wall Street. Clothing shops, accessories, furniture, antiques, lighting, even jewellery stores in the affluent parts of Manhattan, were displaying that same sign and time after time we witnessed removal lorries taking away what was left of somebody's dream enterprise idea in the heart of the city that never sleeps. Strange times indeed.

I flew into America for a family wedding. It's not the first time we have been here. In total I think I have now been in the United States on twelve occasions since I came here first to my sister and brother's homes in the 1980s, but the country we encountered this week is a very different one to the one we met in those olden days. In the run-up to a Presidential election and in the heart of a deeply traumatic stock market collapse, the USA is a place that is full of uncertainties and divisions at the moment. The split in the population is the thing that probably strikes you more than anything else when you come here, not just the divide between the Democrats and the Republicans but the even wider divisions of race and colour that are now more obvious than ever before in the heart of a bitter electoral battle and a nightmare on Wall Street.

New York is pretty safe Democrat territory. Obama is fairly sure to carry the vote here but even within this state there's an unsettling feeling that race may well be the issue across the country that will deny him his place in history as the first black man in the White House. The analysis by the ordinary folk on the streets is scary. "If he wins and makes it to the White House he will be shot, make no mistake about it," the barman tells me without as much as raising an eyebrow in a pub on McLean Avenue in Yonkers. "America can't handle a black man in the top job," I am told repeatedly yet the polls on CNN and in all the mainstream newspapers tell us that this is a country that has matured, come to get over its prejudices and even the prospect of a twenty per cent racial back lash against Obama will not be enough to deny him victory on November 4th.

Uncertainty is everywhere here. For the last seven days McCain has battered the electorate with a continuous barrage of anti-Obama campaigning based on just one slogan thrown out by his opponent. "This man says he wants to spread the wealth," McCain advises his audiences day after day. "That can only mean one thing, taking more money out of your pocket in taxes and that will hit everybody." McCain says it so casually and so unemotionally that I'm consistently surprised by it. 'Spreading the wealth' is apparently now a treasonable offence in the US, bad words to come up with it if you accept his line of thought but clearly his backroom team of gurus and experts have told him that this is the way to go and that the American public will be swayed if not made even fearful by this prospect. He hammers home the same point day after day in the campaign and every time he delivers the words and points again like a robot at some imaginary supporter in his audience the republicans boo and heckle Obama. It's a strange circus based on the realities no doubt of modern life here in the split personality of the United States.

The young man on the ground with the cardboard sign in his hand in front of St. Patrick's Cathedral on 5th avenue doesn't seem to have had wealth or even breakfast shared with him by his fellow Americans for some time. The sign in his arms says 'Homeless and Sleeping In Central Park' and in truth he looks like a man who hasn't seen a bed indoors for some time. America is full of these divisions. Everywhere you look people are losing their homes on a widespread basis. The morning TV shows are full of advice from experts on how to hold onto your house when you can't make the repayments. The advertisement breaks have even more of it, urging the hapless home owners to avail of health insurance and other safety nets if the worst comes to the worst. It all makes for a cheerful sort of a place to be at the moment.

My nephew works for a bank in the city so I reckon, wrongly as it turns out, that he too must have been affected by the downturn and the uncertainty. "Never been busier," he says and I react with incredulity. I don't understand how any of the banks here could be lending money in the present circumstances, but he explains the logic behind it. When the larger banks got into trouble, the safe and profitable business community turned to the smaller institutions with their own fixed assets piled up during the good days. "But who is giving your bank the money to lend?" I ask repeatedly. "We did well when times were good and our assets are still good," he says. "Now we can charge too and our customers know us by our first names so that's better for business!"

The Irish community here is also in a strange place. On McLean avenue in Yonkers they tell me that young people are coming back to America again. The man in charge of Rory Dolan's popular Irish diner says he has seen an upturn in his trade over the last few months, yet the Americans here tell you that jobs are still scarce and money is tight. It's a strange and conflicting tale of two different nations. The Gaelic football teams that were struggling only two years ago to field a side are now back in a healthy state, young unemployed and highly educated students from Ireland returning here in search of the good times as the Celtic Tiger economy's sickness rumbles on at home. "We didn't make use of it when we had it," is a popular comment on the Irish economy among the young couples here who have come back to seek work in America this year. "We had money to burn when the good days rolled in Ireland and we wasted it," a young Leitrim science graduate tells me. "We could have done so much more at home to try and build for a future, yet we squandered it and I'm back in Yonkers to prove it."

At the wedding in La Rochelle I spoke to a man who came out here to work in the States when he was just twenty years old in 1968. He's seen boom and bust on both sides of the Atlantic, yet most of his anger at the moment is targeted at the poor calibre (as he sees it) of all four would-be holders of the highest office in the United States, the candidates on the ticket for the Presidential election. "None of them stands out to me as a well qualified and sound business person that could rescue the country after George W.," he says. "Whoever wins on November 4th is going to have a hell of a job on their hands to get the place back on its feet. My pension is going down the tubes thanks to that man in the White House and, quite frankly, I don't see any of the four coming in as being capable of changing any of that and that's the really sickening part."

Whatever happens on November 4th there's no doubting the scale of the nightmare that still lies ahead for most of the people on this side of the Atlantic. The US economy is so sick that it is now estimated that six out of every ten people here is in debt, something that makes it all the more ironic when you hear such worries about the prospect of one Presidential hopeful 'spreading the wealth' when he gets it! What wealth? The Americans are a deeply depressed race at the moment and it's going to take an awful long time for them to recover from the debacles of Freddie Mac and Fannie Mae. On Broadway on Thursday night one Irish man summed it better than I could. "They live and die by the buck here," he said with a smile on his face. "The only problem is this dollar is mighty sick and may not make it!" Strange and scary times in the USA.

*UPDATE: The 56th election of a President of the United States of America was held on Tuesday, November 4, 2008. Democratic nominee Senator Barack Obama and running mate Senator Joe Biden defeated Republican party nominee Senator John McCain and running mate Governor Sarah Palin. In the end, Obama had a decisive victory over McCain, winning both the popular vote and the electoral college with 365 electoral votes to McCain's 173. He received the largest percentage of the popular vote for a Democrat since Lyndon Johnson in 1964.*

*Obama's response to the financial crisis was largely to try and ensure it never happened again. Rowing in behind regulatory responses to the sub-prime crisis like governments all around the world to try and address the effects of the crisis, he said he wanted to take severe action on lending practices and introduced a series of regulatory proposals in June 2009. He addressed consumer protection, executive pay, bank financial cushions and the sort of capital assets they would be forced to keep on hand from now on, and also enhanced authority for the US Federal reserve to safely wind-down systemically important institutions. In the light of the Lehman Brothers disaster, soft landings were what he really wanted to see in future but not everybody was happy with his efforts.*

*The words 'Going Out of Business' most certainly did not disappear from the shop windows in New York City over Obama's first term in office. It's true that the economy continued to sink for the first six months of his initial term but eventually stability returned to the US markets. And, despite the prediction, Obama was not shot in his first 100 days.*

Chapter 9

# THE BIG FREEZE

John Connell looked out the window from the kitchen of his cottage on Inchboffin island on Lough Ree last Sunday morning and thought that all of his Christmases had come together as a great iron bird appeared in the sky and suddenly began to drop dozens of bales of hay into the field in front of him.

The hovering Aer Corps helicopter slowly but surely came down from the skies and landed to drop off the rest of its badly-needed cargo on the island. But Connell, the quiet and reserved man of the island, hardly flinched as the fierce winds from the giant propellers of the army aircraft sent hay and ice flying in all directions. The seventy-five year old Shannon fisherman and farmer is made of hardy stuff. The day before the bales arrived he had politely told four Gardai who had walked on the ice out to the island (with a boat alongside them) that he would prefer not to accept their invitation to go back with them to the mainland. "I have enough food and supplies to keep me going for another week," John told the Garda Water Unit members, "and anyway I want to keep an eye on the cattle!"

The place held by this decent and shy Westmeath farmer in Irish history is now well assured. As a stockholder who lives permanently on the island, he remains the last full time inhabitant of any of the islands of Lough Ree, a part of this country which has quite rightly found its place in folklore thanks to a deeply-rooted historical theme based on religious grounds. There's something in our psyche which makes it almost impossible not to feel somehow privileged in even walking on some of these islands such has been their fantastic heritage. Island life has always held a fascination for Irish writers and travellers and many the day-dreamer has enjoyed a field day there. Traditionally when we think about island life we think of our off-shore islands, but given that Lough Ree is the third largest lake in Ireland it should come as no surprise to learn that many of our islands sustained small populations of inhabitants right up to modern days. The shores of Lough Ree in Roscommon, Longford and Westmeath are scattered with relatives of people who came from the islands, forced to leave their home and heritage behind them there as electricity came to Ireland in the 1940s, 1950s and even the 1960s, while Mr Connell stuck his heels in and stayed put in Inchboffin.

The basis for making the islands of Lough Ree a protected part of a new national park is still very strong. There is evidence of a ring fort on Inchmore, but many of the islands experienced their initial residential life during the early Christian period when monasteries sprung up in places such as Inchcleraun, better known to us all as the Quaker, in the north of the lake and Hare Island in the south. Many of these monasteries survived (or were revived) in the early medieval period and continued to flourish until the time of Henry VIII when destruction was their fate. The island people of Lough Ree needed to be a hardy race: John Connell didn't lick it off the ground! They eked out a living through fishing and farming. There was nothing romantic about life on the islands, the reality of surviving with the basics there was very tough. During the winter, these small communities were frequently disconnected from the mainland for long stretches, being cut off from shops and pubs was the norm, they were deprived of the services of church and state, and often were unable to get medical assistance. Their means of travel was often an open boat with split-sail and oars and the transport of livestock was a precarious business. Today a handful of holiday homes provide a small injection of life to the islands of Lough Ree in the summer time. A few of them in our part of the lake are still farmed, though the owners now live on the mainland. The islands are all natural sanctuaries, beautiful (even in snow and ice), unspoiled and steeped in tradition and history.

Inchbofin, where John Connell lives, is in the barony of Kilkenny West, the parish of Noughaval and the Poor Law Union of Athlone according to the history books. The island consists of 65 acres, 3 roods and 11 perches and I think we walked across at least ten of those acres last Sunday morning, trying to bring bales of hay to the cattle for John. Like on the Quaker, there are plenty of stone ruins above the ground to prove its historic past. We're told St. Rioch, a contemporary of St. Ciaran's, founded a monastery on Inchbofin in 530 and the remains of two churches survive on the island even today in the frost and snow. The more elaborate of the two churches is at the north-eastern point of the island and it has a most irregular enclosure. To the north of the altar is a fine Romanesque window, and above a window is a bishop's head carved in stone. At a different time in our history this might have been very seriously in danger of being plundered. A robbery on the island of Inchcleraun not so many years back still remains in folklore locally, with tales of an attempted sale to Boston's Jesuits of St. Diarmuid's ancient carved cross firmly in the back of many minds. It didn't take them long to work out where the ancient relic was coming from and a sting was set up within hours. The FBI moved in to carry out arrests the next day, returning later with the loot to Ireland for a lap of honour, stopping at Barley Harbour to meet the media.

The smaller ruin to the south of Inchboffin dates from the 12th or 13th century. Both ruins belong to the monastery of the Canons of St. Augustine which flourished on the island until the general dissolution of the monasteries in the time of Henry VIII. In the midst of such a significant place of heritage it is almost refreshing to hear John Connell talk about his cattle and his sales of stock. "I have thirty head of cattle here now but I wanted to sell a good few of them last November and I couldn't get them out with the floods at the time," he told me on the island that day. "I had hay for them but I couldn't get any more in with the boat so it was great to see the helicopter coming." As soon as the army personnel arrived on Inchboffin soil,

John, who is renowned for being very quiet-spoken and shy, came out and grasped the hand of the Air Corps man in the green boiler suit. "I am very, very grateful for the help," he assured him, "you have given me a great hand at a time when I needed it. You never forgot me"

Travelling back with the helicopter crew to the mainland I don't think I will ever forget the superb aerial view of the great mass of ice between the island and the mainland. At various points around the island there were deep cracks in the cap but for the most part it was just one long never-ending glacier with the island landscape standing out in pale grey alongside the shoreline. Truly breathtaking. Will we ever see it again? Later, as we left the chopper and headed back to Athlone, I asked some of the locals if John Connell would ever return to Glasson to enjoy his retirement. "John has lived all his life on Inchboffin: he will die there now," was the solemn reply from a neighbour, "and part of our heritage will die with him."

*UPDATE: John Connell is alive and well and still living on the island of Inchboffin. He was never a great one for the mobile phone so I rang his good friend Kevin 'Boxer' Moran from Coosan to get the very latest update on the extraordinary life of this great man of the lake. "He's still here farming and nothing has changed since that bad winter," Boxer told me on a day when he himself had set out on a fishing trip to 'Boffin. "He is still the only Irish citizen living permanently on the islands of the lake," Boxer said. "He is farming away. He goes to the mainland on the boat for his groceries whenever he needs to and he is happy with his life." Now in his 80's, Connell's place in history is secure. We may or may not ever meet again, on the street of Glasson or on the next Aer Corps mercy mission with the fodder that may head his way when and if the big freeze returns. But one thing is for sure - we will never meet his likes again.*

Chapter 10

# PRAYING FOR ST ANTHONYS

Breaking News from the Gateway Bar in Great Friar's Street, Reading Town Centre: St. Anthony's Junior Gaelic football club is back in business and trying to win the silverware again. Berkshire's toughest competitors on the London GAA scene are firing on all cylinders, having already won a league title and are now into the championship semi-final again. Three cheers for the tide of emigration!

Over the last twenty years I have written several times about the fate of the Anthony's Junior club in Reading. With a brother-in-law living in the area and closely associated with the team for the best part of fourteen years, my wife Angela and I have seen the rise and fall of this tiny little London GAA club throughout that period as we spent a few days in the UK visiting him and his family from time to time since as far back as 1997. At this stage you might say we see ourselves as lifetime supporters of the local GAA club there, yet its progress up and down the leagues over the course of nearly two decades, often hovering near extinction, has been inextricably linked to the economic progression and recession on this emerald isle. It really is a fascinating story of the survival of the Irish on foreign soil.

Our annual visits to the Anthony's games down at their ground in the Kings Meadow public park near the railway station in Reading have been famous for their entertainment. Twenty five years ago this was a small junior club with only a handful of young players on their books when the first tide of emigration from here in the late 1980's sent a great stock of young talented and highly capable Gaelic footballers into the club. They arrived in Reading and London in search of jobs when their own country was unable to provide them with a livelihood, working in construction, healthcare, IT and even road maintenance, yet when their day's work was done with they all seemed to find the attraction as strong as ever to come and wanted to be part of a GAA club again many miles from their home parish, and struggling St. Anthony's was only too pleased to open their doors and welcome them in.

Jobs for the Irish in healthcare was always something the Anthony's specialised in. On Reading's Oxford Road, club stalwarts gathered for the weekly Sunday game TV viewings, as well as regular meetings and get-togethers at The Wishing Well Pub. But there was another strong Irish reason to be in that area: only yards away, dozens of young men and women were coming to England to do their training to become nurses in the shadow of the city's historic Royal Hospital. On our visits over those years we met men and women from Mayo, Dublin, Cavan, Leitrim, Roscommon and Longford on almost every occasion, young people who wanted to pursue a career in healthcare in their native land but were not afforded the opportunity to do so at home and found the British nation more than willing to take them in and give them that education. The Wishing Well as a result was always a hectic spot, a crossroads in England where the nurse from Dublin met the builder or plumber from Mayo, where the brickie from Cork played cards or darts against the chippy from Carlow and where all human life existed. With new blood and fresh energy St. Anthony's flourished throughout that period. The club went from strength to strength, bringing home silverware for the first time in years and starting to coach young schoolboys in the skills of Gaelic football for the very first time in their English communities.

In more recent times we have been back in Reading when the club's progression went into reverse. The Celtic Tiger was bad for the Anthony's. Scratch that, it was even worse, the Tiger was brutal for the club. The footballers went home in their droves as the Irish economy grew, leaving behind this little junior club in Reading to fend for itself as their young stars returned to their native parishes to work in the Irish building sites and hospitals for a change. The club hit another black patch in its history and playing numbers declined. The age profile of the team went up again and the matches down at Kings Meadow were often physical encounters where often a row with the referee would be the only entertaining highlight of the game.

Last Saturday I am glad to report that the Kings Meadow was a transformed arena once again, however, when we turned up to watch St. Anthony's face Robert Emmets of London in a very entertaining Intermediate championship encounter. Walking into the GAA pitch from the car park along the river Thames I wasn't even sure at first if I was in the right football park. Wearing their customary sky blue the Anthony's were in flying form. Attacking up the wings in waves these young footballers seemed to have hit top gear again. They played one-two's, ran on in support for their colleagues, caught the ball cleanly in the area and, more significantly than anything else, scored with both their left and right feet when it suited them throughout the match. An entirely new stock of young footballers from Ireland has obviously arrived.

The evolution of the club is, of course, once again down to what has happened to the Irish economy. The age profile of the players arriving here from Ireland every week is in their early 20's – young, well educated men and women from all over the country - Roscommon clubs Eire Og and Clann na Gael included - and for the most part young footballers who had hoped to stay at home with their families to make a living on Irish soil but have been given little option but to emigrate and are now turning to the GAA once again to give them a sense of belonging where their new lives are beginning. The really fascinating thing for me to see was the way that history is indeed repeating itself in such an amazing way. After a comprehensive victory on Saturday the players went back to the pub in the town now owned by Martin O'Sullivan, a genial Corkman who was the former proprietor of The Wishing Well on the Oxford Road all those years ago and, as they chatted about the match, passed around the lotto tickets for the GAA club and munched their sandwiches, in walked a batch of six young trainee nurses from the midlands and throughout the north east, our emigrants back into the same Irish community that their predecessors had to visit over twenty five years ago in the last recession and back looking for jobs and perhaps even romance here, meeting many of the young Irish men they used to meet at home.

Leaving Reading on Monday I was told by the St. Anthony's treasurer that the dinner dance this year is going to be a 'must-not-miss' event when it comes around in November. "We have already won silverware in the league," he told me, pointing to a trophy sitting on the sideboard in the bar. "With the championship semi-final coming up in two weeks time I think our name is on the cup. We are back in business again and this time we have the young lads to sustain it if the club could be promoted up to senior rank in a few years."

It surely is an ill wind that does not give somebody in this world the benefit of some misfortune. The rise and fall and rise of the Anthony's is essentially a story of Irish emigration and its knock-on benefits for the world, not just the UK, and we were proud to see this story from the other side of the Irish Sea last week as the fairytale begins all over again for one club and its loyal band of supporters and officials. Come on the Anthony's!

*UPDATE: St. Anthony's GAA Club was formed in 1963 by a group of like-minded and very proud Reading-based Irishmen (a lot of them Mayo natives) who were determined to create a GAA club in the Reading area so players simply wouldn't have to get a train to London to play every weekend. The club's very first championship winning team was made up , almost entirely, of men from the parish of Kilmaine in county Mayo. After many years of struggling to field a side, how proud this group of founding members would surely have been if they had been around over the 2013, 2014 and 2015 seasons as the modern-day wearers of the club's sky blue* colours have mixed it with the best at both men's and women's level football in London - and won plenty of titles. The latest triumph came just at the end of September 2015 when the Anthony's Junior side staged the most remarkable of journeys to glory in the London championship with a drawn semi-final, a replay victory and then a stunning county junior final success over St. Clarets at the London GAA Grounds in Ruislip.

There's always a really unusual atmosphere about Ruislip: every time I go there I feel it's a bit like being at a fleadh in Ennis with all these counties represented away from home, but Sunday September 27th, 2015 was particularly special. On a day some readers may remember Ireland playing their second game in the Rugby World Cup at Wembley supporters of St. Anthony's had a double booking with the club taking part in yet another historic London football final. The opponents this time were Uxbridge-based St. Clarets and the prospects were not particularly promising for the Berkshire based boys, trailing on a score line of 1-8 to three points with 13 minutes played in the second half. What happened next was extraordinary, the Irish lads from Reading scoring one goal and six points without reply from their opponents during the remainder of the match to walk away with the cup.

The scenes of celebration in London and Reading were really emotional to watch and I couldn't help but think of the pioneering work done for them by people like Mick Lenihan, Eoin O'Connell, Conor McGreevy and Eamonn O'Reilly in recent years. These hardy souls put out teams to play football when the Celtic Tiger was roaring and their numbers were fiercely depleted. Now, like the club's successful and all conquering ladies team, they were back winning titles and a new underage side for the 'parish' is also making steady progress. This is what makes the GAA great in our society, the bond that keeps us together as the Irish no matter where we go, and I can't wait to get back to the Kings Meadow to see the next performance of the new champions. Come on the Anthony's - there's no stopping you now.

Chapter 11

# You're on Air!

I used to be a shareholder in Shannonside local radio, so I suppose you could say I have paid more attention than most to its progress over the course of the last twenty years as it made its way into commercial life and played an important part in the social and community diary of the people of this part of the country.

I bought my shares in Shannonside during one of the fledgling station's many cash calls in its troubled early years. I was a member of staff with the fancy title of Head of News (we had 3 people in the newsroom!) when the then chief executive John Morrin, a brilliant radio man with fantastic energy, approached four of us in the management team of the station to put up some cash and help kickstart the station's financial progress. I was asked to go in with John himself, Pat Kennedy the Sales Manager, Jimmy Naughton , the technical supremo and Morning show host Joe Finnegan.

I don't know about the rest of them but I borrowed the money to take my share and duly sat at the board room table for about a year to see why Shannonside wasn't exactly making a million every month. It was very much a learning curve for me, as one of the Irish Catholic bishops might put it! We continued to struggle on the financial front and, even before I left to go to RTE when the job offer came, there were indications that the station might not survive unless its main shareholder at that stage, Patrick 'Buddy' Kiernan from Cavan, bailed it out at the bank.

Most people in this part of the country won't have known this but in those early days Shannonside was owned pretty much in its entirety by Buddy Kiernan, a hugely successful Kilnaleck business man with thousands of pigs and a very successful mill for making pig feed near Granard. Kiernan, a staunch Fine Gael supporter, was an expert businessman. He nominated Peter Brady, the then Chairman of Cavan county GAA Board, to represent him on the board of the company and, at a later stage, his own son came in as a temporary managing director. They were both excellent businessmen.

Attending board meetings was always a strange experience for me. Brady was the consummate diplomat in the chair but around the room there were people with very different agendas. In one corner you had the businessmen who were being asked again to put in money to keep the place afloat and obviously wanted to see some sort of progress being made to getting a return on their investments. On the other side there was usually at least one representative of the churches because, even though most people didn't know it, the local diocese also had shares in the operation. Under the guidance of the local bishops, they too had forked out to take a place at the table when local radio was born in the late 80's. Of course their interest was not just a commercial one. I think they also wanted a slice of the action because they had hoped to impose some sort of a religious ethos on the station and its audience. Without demanding it and jumping up or down, they had a strong influence in those days. Their weekly religious programme went out to a sizeable local audience. They had the daily angelus bell ringing and they also had their Sunday morning mass or service broadcast live. Maybe they would have been listened to anyway but, with shares in the company and a seat at the boardroom table, they had strong influence in Shannonside. And it was a healthy one too.

I wasn't a staff member with Shannonside when it started in 1989 so I can't really comment on those very early days but I have fond memories of a period in the early 1990s when I did work there, having been asked to move by John Morrin from my job in the Cavan Leader. For the previous year I had worked with journalist Niall Delaney on a weekend current affairs show called 'Primetime' that had gone down well. We poked our nose into politics and commercial life and exposed one or two practices that were not doing anyone any credit, but it was when I joined the staff on a fulltime basis that I realised how powerful a medium local radio was and how crucial it was to the people of the local community.

These were the halcyon days of Shannonside FM. Broadcasters Kathryn Doherty (who died tragically in an accident some years later) and afternoon host Grace Brennan (Grace & Guests) put out new and creative daily show material in the arts and current affairs areas that gave women in the Shannonside area a voice for the first time. DJs Peter Casey and Joe Finnegan built up a great rapport with their audience with a mixture of chat and craic, and sports presenter Seamus Duke's gaelic games commentaries always were well informed and always went down well. Benny O'Brien gave a great Longford flavour to the sport at the weekends. The late Frank Young put a serious amount of effort into a weekly farming programme and Fr. John Cullen from Ballybay church in Kiltoom and Sister Elizabeth Manning from the Convent of Mercy in Longford did the religious show every week. (We soon nicknamed it 'The God Slot' every Thursday!)

The newsroom was made up of Anne Norris, Jill Hewitt and myself while Tom Lyons from Newtownforbes provided the technical expertise.

Fortunately for us this period also coincided with the election of Rooskey's Albert Reynolds to the office of Taoiseach so we had great political coverage, door stepping the then leader of the Government in his constituency every Monday. Shannonside and Northern Sound built up a reputation for fair and balanced news coverage and the local and general elections brought marathon broadcasts for the first time that gave local radio a huge audience. I think the longer it went on the more I realised, however, that Shannonside's real strength was not in the so-called 'stars' or celebs it made or the waffle that emerged from the egos that sat in the radio studios but the 24 hour nature of the service it provided and its ability to look out for Mrs Brady's missing black and white cat in Elphin minutes after Albert Reynolds had discussed the Northern Ireland peace process on the same show.

The daily reading of the obituaries is a case in hand. Some of the professional national radio stations may have initially laughed at the sombre music and the ads for the headstones that followed the list of daily death notices but the service was a valuable contribution to the local audience, many of whom were elderly and may have been living in isolated rural areas far from local paper shops.

Today Shannonside is a very different organ to the one that I worked for. Many of the old features and the original reporting staff are gone. For commercial reasons, the station's merger with the Cavan–Monaghan station means that you are likely to hear as many requests for somebody from Carrickmacross or Castleblaney than you are for your neighbour down the road but this is perhaps the price that had to be paid for survival. For me the station doesn't get out enough to the local communities any more on news outside broadcasts when the local stories happen. I remember brilliant shows produced by the late Kathryn Doherty and Seamus Duke when Kilmore Post office closed and the meat factory in Ballaghaderreen burnt down, but broadcaster Mary Claire Greally and her colleagues in the newsroom today are working under different budgets and have made their mark in different ways with important news stories and good journalism.

The sale of the business to Kerry Radio made a nice few bob for many of those who had forked out more money on several occasions down the years when times were bad but, alas, yours truly had sold his shareholding long before that. I remain proud, however, of my days there and the programs we made and I also congratulate all who have worked there over the course of the last 20 years on what they have done for the radio audience. They can justifiably take a bow on this special birthday. Here's to 20 more years!

*UPDATE: Shannonside/Northern Sound has just celebrated its 25th anniversary. The regional focus continues and the audiences have grown over that period. Peter Casey now broadcasts regularly on Midlands Radio 3. Seamus Duke is to be heard on Mid West Radio and Deirdre Kelly, who also worked with me towards the end of my time in Shannonside, is an occasional broadcaster on Mid West radio in Ballyhaunis. The reputation of the station as a good training camp for broadcasters is still intact. From my short period there a number of reporters have joined the national airwaves. Damian O'Reilly, Fran McNulty, James Healy, Fintan Duffy and Sinead Hussey are all to be heard on RTE radio or TV while Niall Donnelly, Gareth O'Connor, Audrey Carville, Declan McBennett and Pauline McKenna, who worked on the Northern Sound end of the network, have all gone on to successful careers with UTV,Today FM, RTE and BBC.*

Chapter 12

# THE MAN FROM CLARE

"Bart is dead." In the course of a telephone call lasting only a couple of minutes on a quiet Thursday afternoon in July, the blunt news hit home that the former principal of Lanesborough Vocational School, my alma mater, has passed away after taking ill very suddenly while on a shopping mission in Longford with his wife Bernadette. Most of us knew that Mr Clancy, as we addressed him formally all those years ago at 'the Tech', had retired some time back after a long and devoted career as both teacher and principal, but we had also seen him around the town, in church and at the odd furniture auction looking as sprightly and active as ever. He remained full of the joys of life and keen as ever to look back at those formative days of education in the old technical school, which later assumed the title of a vocational school in the 70's, and went on to become the community college after its amalgamation with the convent. No matter how the name has changed, however, the association of this proud Clare man with the the progressive development of this institution and the many hundreds of young men and women who successfully went through it will never be mistaken.

A native of Kilfearagh, Kilkee in County Clare, Bart helped to steer a couple of generations of us young people from Lanesborough, Ballyleague, Ballagh, Cashel, Cloontagh, Curraghroe, Kilrooskey and Cloontuskert areas through second level education, a dedicated and dutiful teacher who took many the young student under his

**BACK TO THE FUTURE**

– 75 –

wing, helped form character, and guided them towards a profession or a career best suited, but perhaps not always immediately apparent, to them. He was also an enforcer who steered the school to a higher level of excellence, took his role as head of discipline seriously, and went more than just an extra mile to put students and staff on a different academic level.

My memories of Bart are based mainly on early school trips to the Spring Show in the RDS and in particular our very first excursion outside of Ireland when he led a group of very giddy students to the UK and France in the early 1980's. At the time it was all a bit of an adventure for teenagers like us, but I still can recall the meticulous level of organisation that he put into the trip and the many hours we sat in his technical drawing classes talking about preparations. He seemed to look forward to the excursion as much as we did, loving to travel and keen to see new things and meet different people. He may have cautioned us about how we were to behave on our boat trips across the Irish Sea and on to France, but he never went overboard about the discipline issue and concentrated instead on making sure we saw all the main sights of London and Paris and really enjoyed the trip along the way. It turned out to be a fantastic school tour expertly guided by Sheelagh Stafford whose fluent French made everything so much easier, and I think Bart enjoyed it even more than us.

I still have a few grainy colour pictures of the school tour, fond memories of our bus driving down the Mall and around Buckingham Palace, and I am pleased to say that we discussed that trip again when the Class of 1984 met for our 25th year reunion at the Lifebelt Bar in Ballyleague at Christmas in 2009. We were not to know it then, but we were saying thanks to Bart for the very last time. We laughed a lot also to recall the late-night walk as a group from our Paris hostel that wasn't really supposed to bring us through the red light district on the way to a skating rink at the end of the first day on French soil. These and many other fond memories of five busy years at the Tech were passed around the room that night.

Bart Clancy's lasting legacy will be the fact that he steered a new school on a consistent path of progress when he took over as Principal more than forty years ago. Although he had retired by January 2007, he was a very proud man when then Minister for Education and Science, Micháel Martin, officially opened the new extension at the school. Hundreds of young men and woman owe a great debt of gratitude to Bart Clancy for the very significant difference he has made to their lives. When you're a teenager full of great plans for the world, a fair bit of rebellion and a good share of youthful exuberance, it's something you don't really buy into at that stage in your life. Students are rarely fans of their Principal and we were hardly too pleased to see Bart breaking up our successful mitch of a religion class in Gill's Fields at one stage in those years, but we later realised that Bart's best interests were ours and he meant well in everything he did at the Tech.

Today the students there are educated in bright, spacious and modern facilities and Bart should rightfully take the praise for so much of that. It was a very long way from 1953 when the late Ger Farrell (father of Adrian/ grandfather of Gerald), secretary of the Lanesborough Development Committee wrote to the Longford VEC asking them to provide a technical school in the area to cater for the needs of the young people. It was the start of an exciting new era for the area and a whole new generation of people had to be educated and prepared for something the previous generation certainly knew very little about, a rewarding and well-paid full-time local job with Bord na Mona or the ESB. Bart was instrumental in putting the apprenticeship courses at the heart of the weekly activity at the new Lanesborough Vocational School. Hundreds of people from all over the country came to the school to complete the training that went with their new apprenticeship and dozens of people were given solid advice and encouragement to start out on a career as a fitter or an electrician that progressed them to immediate and longstanding employment.

When Micheál Martin opened the extension that day in 2007, the first Principal, Tom Moloney returned to meet up again with Bart Clancy and so many other former members of the staff. It was a special occasion and great tales were told. In the church yard outside St. Mary's in Lanesborough last July, we spoke again to many more former members of the staff and past pupils who also shared great memories of those days from the past, but above all remembered Bart with feelings of great respect and deep fondness. 'Bart' may be gone from this earth but his family can be all be very proud of his achievements and the lasting difference he made in that community. The US magazine publisher Malcolm Forbes said, "Education's purpose is to replace an empty mind with an open one." That Bart achieved this and much more is beyond any doubt.

# Chapter 13

# LETTER TO EOGHAN

Dear Son,

I know you are just four weeks old today and, despite your very smart arrival into this world, you will hardly be able to read this. But I am taking this opportunity to put a few things down in print so that in time to come you can look back with the help of your old grey-haired father on this very week (and this newspaper column) and perhaps it might remind you of the point in history when your future was partially decided by a very stressed out Irish Government in the midst of one of the greatest financial messes the country (and the world) has ever seen. The main thing that will probably decide part of your destiny in the coming week is the budget. As your father I have to give it to you straight. The bad news comes first, so let's get it out of the way. If the weekend newspapers are to be believed, it would appear that the allowance paid to your mother for your welfare every month is going to be one of the first major casualties of the recession. 'Informed sources' in government seem to have tried to break the ice with almost every newspaper going by talking of a cut of ten per cent in the children's allowance in Wednesday's budget.

Don't be surprised if the actual cut in your monthly allowance is a wee bit less. It's an old trick in political circles, used by Government parties of all persuasions over the years. If there's going to be bad news in the budget for one particularly vulnerable section of people you get the word out early and try and ease the fall, so to speak. If they are briefing the press that it is going to be a ten per cent cut then chances are when the Finance Minister actually stands up to make the speech it will probably be a couple of percentage points less than that, leaving us all supposedly a bit 'relieved' when it happens that the attack on the money in our pocket is not just as bad as they had made it out to be but leaves us poorer nonetheless than we were this time last week. It's all part of this psychology that has been used every year since time memorial in Leinster House and, if I sound a bit cynical, then it's because maybe I have become that way over all those years before you came along.

However, there is one saving grace in all of this for you, young man. It actually might not happen at all. Long long ago, before your mother and father ever got married, there was another man who was the Minister for Finance in a Government under pressure and he tried to change something that affected the welfare of children in a fairly dramatic way too. That man's name was John Bruton and he actually proposed some sort of a tax on children's shoes in a bid to raise more money for a cash-starved Government. It all happened at a time that is probably not that different to where we are now in history because those times were really tough and that government was also relying on the support of a handful of independent TDs to hold onto their place in power. So when the row broke out about the attempt to put a tax on a child's shoe, an unmerciful furore was kicked up and eventually the independent TD withdrew his support from the budget. Not only did the budget not make it, but the Government fell.

In due course you will realise that everything is never really black and white in this world you have just recently joined. Political commentators in the national media are now quietly predicting that this very same 'car-crash' scenario could very well happen this week if Brian Cowen's luck turns really bad. I heard one print journalist on the radio on Saturday predicting there are at least five windy backbench TDs in Fianna Fail and two in the Greens who could well cut and run to the country if the smell from the budget unveiled by Brian Lenihan on Wednesday is much worse than anything that ever emanated from any of your nappies! The political mindset for these TDs is fairly simple:

by refusing to accept a particular measure that would badly effect the welfare of any of their constituents they could easily vote against the budget and the Government, and then run back to their constituency to remind all the people who voted for them how worried they are about their welfare and why they should be immediately given a place on the very top of the moral ground in the county and then be returned unopposed in the next general election. It's an old trick and one that is usually quite successful, though not always 100 per cent effective. When you look this week at the number of Dail deputies who have built their support for Brian Cowen's government around deals and wish lists for their constituency and then you consider how bad a state the nation is in, it's not hard to see how the whole house of cards could come crumbling down around the Clara man's ears and have us all heading for the polls in a general election sooner rather than later.

Lots of other Mammies and Daddies will be feeling pretty sick on Wednesday. Cutting the children's allowance will undoubtedly annoy and affect many parents if it happens this week, especially those with more than three or four young children in childcare and are heavily dependent on the monthly allowance to pay for the creche costs and all the other modern day bills that go with it. But I suppose my other concerns for you, young son, this week are based on a somewhat bigger picture (you are only four weeks old after all) and what effect the budget on Wednesday could have on the long term outlook for you in the country you grow up to try and live in after another 20 years.

A word of advice for a young man like you heading into the big bad world: beware of flashy new words and theories coming from politicians. We are always hearing this terrific new phrase that talks about the Government creating 'a stimulus package' at the moment. The slaughter of the value of banking shares and the decline of the construction sector have been two of the most depressing developments in this troubled country in the last three years and any parent must really wonder with salary levels sliding how they will pay for important things such as education for their children in future. If the nation is to ever again try and create anything like full employment then many believe that only a recovery of mammoth proportions in the construction sector will bring this about. For all of its failures the building sector is one of the few areas where many young men a little older than you at this stage could make a living and be able to stay on in this country. Without it their future is undoubtedly abroad, a very sad fact for hundreds of families, so it is fair for me to wonder when and how this particular industry can be turned around before you get to the stage when you might need a job there too or have to turn your back on your native land. Your mother and brother and I would have a major problem with that.

I think it's fair to say we are all hoping for a bit more optimism about the future and the world you will live in when the budget happens this week. Brian Lenihan will be expected by many people not only to plug the hole in the nation's finances but help to create some sort of a feeling of recovery for the future. How many times have we heard people bemoan the fact recently that they have not been told enough times that there is a future for our children when all of this belt-tightening is over? How many times have we heard graduates seek reassurances that we will be able to invest in the so-called smart economy in the tough days ahead and therefore ensure that there is a future for thousands of them in their chosen profession? Many parents like myself will look to this budget therefore to create a very real feeling that the nation is ready to try and be at the cutting edge when the recovery does eventually start.

The next ten years will undoubtedly be a tough time for many sectors. You're a lucky man you will only be relaxing in national school throughout this time. In the past we have always talked with some confidence about the presence of Hewlett Packard and Dell in this country and the firm foundations given to the IT sector. Youngsters like you will be heading in their thousands to IT's and third level institutions over the course of the next twenty years, but the closure of Dell has shaken many parents and what happens in the next few months may well decide which path in life or chosen profession that will be pushed in your direction when you head to school. Several other key decisions in the budget on Wednesday may even change the fate of your own lifestyle. If more money goes on the price of a pack of cigarettes or a pint of beer this week you can be sure your mother and father will certainly be leaving both of them on the "out of bounds" list for you until the next recovery is well underway. Taxing the well off will not hit your pocket money (because neither your mother nor your father are in that category), but if the price of petrol or diesel goes up you might be facing a few more days than expected in your own playroom instead of elsewhere.

One final issue should be of fairly key importance to you, young man. Any attempt to reduce the weekly pension paid to the retired folk of this country will be looked on in a very poor light by your parents on Wednesday. Apart from our obvious concerns for the implications of this on your grandad's Christmas present fund, an accountant told me recently that the only thing assured after the downturn in the economy and the appalling decline in government income over the last five years was that after 2020 your parents would be working until they were at least seventy before they would even qualify for the old age pension. On top of that, if pension payments start to go down instead of up this week we will both be pretty bad company for you over the next twenty years. And that can only mean one thing: no pocket money either.

So, by all means enjoy this budget day, Mr Eoghan Mullooly. Please try not to pay too much attention to some of the language your parents might use towards the television when the big man with the budget speech is standing up on Wednesday evening. And remember, there's plenty of time for this great little country to recover so that you can enjoy a long and prosperous life with your friends here. The future may look just a little bleak with talk of global warming, hairshirt budgets and flood water coming in but, look on the bright side, the man in the red coat with the white beard will be here one way or the other to see you on Christmas Eve, and there's no VAT on his presents this year either.

*UPDATE: The leaks were accurate. In the 2009 budget, then finance Minister Brian Lenihan cut back on child benefit. For the first two children, the rate was cut from €166 a month to €150 for each child. If you had more than 2 children, the amount you received for the additional ones was cut from €203 to €187. Twelve months later, with the nation's finances still in dire straits, children and their parents were hit again. This time there was a €10 per month cut for the first and second child. The rate for the 3rd and subsequent child was €37 higher than the first 2 children, but then the difference was cut so that the third child rate went to just €27 higher than the rate for child 1 and 2. In 2012, it happened again. This time the rate was cut by €19 a month for the third child to €148 and by €17 for 4th and subsequent children to €160. Somewhere in the middle of these cuts on families, Brian Lenihan's tenure as Finance Minister came to an end, Brian Cowan was unceremoniously removed from office, and Fianna Fail and the Greens were kicked out of Government.*

*The combined effects of the cuts was to have a severe effect on thousands of families, with childcare agencies warning that drastic cuts would condemn families on the breadline to a life of poverty, hunger and homelessness. Children's rights activist Norah Gibbons claimed that cuts on those surviving on low incomes and social welfare would result in many children going without one full meal every week, and many did. Eoghan Mullooly also felt the effects of the budget cuts, but not as badly as others. His parents were lucky to have two good jobs and they knew it. Even though child benefit was restored to some extent over the last two years, some families are still in that poverty trap with loans and debts all around them and for them this nightmare is continuing. Spiraling debt has taken its toll on families in every corner of the country and it will take more than just two budgets to end the ordeal for many.*

*Brian Lenihan died at the age of 52 from pancreatic cancer on 10 June 2011.*

# Chapter 14

# THE CRUELTY OF NATURE

It's a Saturday evening and, after what seems like a month of very pleasant weather with a great deal of sunshine and hardly a shower of decent rain in weeks, I am standing on one of the fingers of the new jetties at the Waterways Ireland marina in Ballyleague trying to take cover from a squawl of rainfall while waiting for a lift from a passing vessel.

The destination this evening is to be Inchmcdermott Island on Lough Ree, one of the smallest islands on the lake or indeed the entire Shannon system and a drop-off point that is no more than ten or fifteen minutes away on the boat we are going on. The mission today is a somewhat strange one. I have never before set foot on Inchmcdermott in my travels on the lake or the Shannon, but over the weekend several locals have reported to me that upwards on twenty members of the island's herd of wild goats have died in mysterious circumstances. The actual detail of how the animals have died is confused between tales of gunshot wounds and other ailments, so I am glad to be able to leave the lakeshore behind and head south towards the 'cut' in the shannon navigation and out onto the top of the Lake of Kings.

Our skipper is John Fayne of the Lough Ree Sub Aqua club. A man who has lived on the shoreline of the Shannon himself for all of his life, Fayne knows every nook and cranny of the lake and is an expert tour guide for the mission ahead. (One or two of the rocks in the lake he even knows personally, but that's another story!) He carefully steers the sturdy rigid inflatable boat with the distinctive orange colour and its gigantic outboard engine out of the bay and into the wide expanses of the lake where we are now all of a sudden the main target of the elements. Heavy wind and rain batters the crew who turn north for protection as the boat picks up speed, but within ten minutes we are safely mooring at Inchmcdermott the first half of this adventure behind us.

Inchmcdermott is the first island of any major size on Lough Ree that crops up on the navigation line heading south from the bridge at Lanesborough towards the town of Athlone. After passing the red and black navigation markers in the 'cut', and the next set a few hundred yards further along, the small island comes quickly into focus with a distinctive tree on the lakeshore that is decked out with not one but about twenty five bird nests. To the right of the island is Ferrinch, another small piece of isolated land in the Shannon, and further south one can also get a glimpse of Goat Island, Bushy Island, Little Island and eventually Inchenagh, the only real substantial one of the five we have seen so far today if truth is to be told. I think it's fair to say that I know this area reasonably well. I have been out in Inchenagh on several occasions over the last forty years. My late father was a very good friend of Jimmy Shea, a popular postman and farmer whose family have been closely associated with island life for decades on Lough Ree. The first memory of going by boat out to Inchenagh when I was still in national school is the sight of all the wild goats there, a sight that I recalled two weeks earlier when I passed by the same clutch of five islands on a cruiser and once again spotted the dozens of wild animals grazing there.

The first report that there was something wrong with the herd of wild goats in Inchmcdermott came on Friday afternoon. A local fisherman who took refuge on the island soon came across the first of what he said were more than twenty carcasses strewn across the narrow terrain and became alarmed by what had happened. By the time we set foot on Inchmcdermott on Saturday night the story has grown some legs on it, more than forty goats had now been shot, one local man told me, and the small island was being painted as being something akin to the last shoot-out at the OK Corral. Seeing is believing, or so they say, so we continued on our journey. With daylight still well on our side we walked slowly from the lakeshore to the first visible carcass just after half past seven. The goat that was on the ground looked like a fairly aged specimen with long sharp horns flowing from its head. A few yards away a second animal that was not quite so old also lay on the ground and, in a clearing nearby, the rest of the group had spotted another five goats lying prostrate on the grassland. Over the course of another fifteen minutes, the six of us counted up to twenty-four dead goats, all of them in a state of reasonable condition, at least to a layperson's eye, and in another part of the island nine live animals were also discovered grazing. Looking closely at the animals, we could not see any obvious injury or cause for their condition. Conscious of the reports that some of the animals had been shot we looked carefully for evidence of wounds or pellets but there was none on any of them, with the possible exception of one animal identified nearby with what looked like a small bullet wound to its head.

The ironic thing about the state of the dead goats was the fact that almost each and everyone of them was lying in a very healthy mop of fresh grass. It has been suggested by some that many of the animals had died from starvation during the bad weather this year, but from what we saw on Saturday it was difficult to understand how so many animals could all have died around the same time. Because of their condition we felt very sure that these deaths have only taken place in the last two weeks or so, long after the growth of grass had re-started on most agricultural land. I am certainly not a veterinary surgeon and would not be qualified in any way to comment on animal nutrition, but all of those around me on Saturday could see that many of the animals seemed to have been quite heavy in weight, they had plenty of flesh there too, and it seemed unlikely to us that they were starving to death.

On the Monday afternoon a spokesman for the Department of Agriculture confirmed that their officials had been asked by a local fisherman to visit the island and had seen for themselves two of the goats that were in a very poor condition. These animals were subsequently put down by the department staff. While grass levels were low on the island at that stage, new growth was evident and a judgment was made that the grazing critical for the herd was returning and would help to restore feed levels for the remaining animals. Another piece of the jigsaw fell into place later on the Monday when the ISPCA also confirmed that they were to visit the island to try and get to grips with the reports they had also received and try to determine how the remainder of the animals had died.

Leaving Inchmcdermott on that Saturday night I still couldn't work out what had happened and thought back to the day at Christmas when the Air Corps had helped bring fodder to sheep and cattle on an island near Glasson. A huge effort had been made to save those animals from starvation and it worked. At the end of the day, we are talking about the death of just twenty goats on this remote island on Lough Ree, and animals that for the most part have run wild for all of their time on this earth. Some would say the cruelty of nature caught up with them in the last few weeks and that is the way nature works, but others are not so sure. "Nature is a tough business," one local farmer reminded me on Monday. "That's the way it has always been. The weather is the biggest enemy for every living beast on those islands. It takes its toll every single day of the year." With local farming having ceased on these islands more than fifteen years ago, the welfare of the wild goats was always going to be a matter for Mother Nature to resolve itself he argued firmly. But should it have been different? Perhaps somebody somewhere could have found time to take all those animals from this isolated spot and have them humanely put down? Perhaps somebody should have cared?

UPDATE: *John Fayne died at a tragically young age on the 14th of October 2012. The loss was greatest for his wife Mary and their family. He worked tirelessly to make their life a better place and successfully built up a dairy farm and a beautiful homestead at Cullentra on the banks of the Shannon. He was hugely popular when he turned to a career at the Innis Ree nursing home in Ballyleague but it was his devotion as a volunteer to the community in which he lived that will be remembered longest. John was centrally involved in the development of the Lough Ree Sub Aqua club. He spent hours and hours 'literally' building up that club, collecting money for their activities and supporting rescues around the country.*

*It was during the course of that work that he picked up the most grevious of injuries to himself after hitting a rock on the waters of Lough Ree. I can still remember the state he was in when Angela and I went to visit him at the Merlin Park Hospital in Galway. Having to be spoon-fed while all his body seemed to be in plaster or propelled from the air. He was still in remarkably good spirits and talking about the next community project to be undertaken. I worked with John for nearly ten years in the Lough Ree Summer School and Co-op hall where we not only managed to stop a very valuable old building being sold to the private sector but we raised thousands of euros to reburbish the place, fit it out with new windows, a heating system and repaired roofs and kitted out new areas. We ran auctions and draws and multiple fundraisers and I don't believe John Fayne ever missed a day when help was needed.*

*It was hardly surprising then that, on the weekend before he died John was still supporting the local community at a GAA event in Dublin, such was the nature of the man.*

*It is fitting that John's name now adorns the walls of the new Lough Ree Sub Aqua club house building in Lanesborough. Gone but not forgotten.*

Chapter 15

# LOCAL HERO

"A politician thinks about the next election; a statesman thinks of the next generation." American theologian and author James Freeman Clarke's words were aptly printed in the requiem mass booklet at the state funeral of former Taoiseach Albert Reynolds. "There's no votes in the North," he himself said many times in his long career yet, when historians sit down in years to come and write up the Rooskey man's final legacy, it will be his stalwart work in the Six Counties, the Downing Street declaration, and the remarkable achievement in bringing everybody to the table to talk about peace in the run-up to the first IRA ceasefire, that will surely stand out amongst his greatest days.

I first encountered Albert Reynolds in the build-up to the 1977 general election. My parents were not exactly Fianna Fail activists but they supported Paddy Farrell from Newtowncashel, a local who collected the milk cans to bring to the creamery. When Paddy ran for the party in the county council elections, it was inevitable we would also be targeted to 'give the vote to Albert' when the time came. I recall seeing him perform at an after-Mass meeting outside St. Mary's Church in Lanesborough, very tanned and in a white trench coat, mobbed by an excited party faithful circling him in the wind and the rain as he spoke about what he would achieve in the Dail if elected. In those days, I could not understand the showbiz element of the event, nor why grown men like Tom McGrath, David Sheeran and John Hester (all now deceased), or young enthusiasts like Michael Reilly and the late Lorcan Connaughton, swarmed around the man pulling fiercely

Mollie Gilleran from Clonkeel, Killashee, county Longford came to Killinure, Lanesborough to make a new life and reared a family of six (including the author). Three of her sisters emigrated to Birmingham but kept in touch with Ireland and sent home their offspring on summer holidays. Pictured: (left to right, behind their mother) Donal, Rose and Eithne Mullooly . To the right, visiting cousins Anne and Frances Lees are pictured with another first cousin Des Nash. The brown bags of cattle meal and nuts in the photograph came from Thomas Newmans and were an important element of Dan Mullooly's farm requirements. The author is suitably armed for the occasion in the front of the photo with the Killinure dog known as 'Fan'.

In an era before the invention of pre-school the Girls National School beside the ESB Power station in Lanesborough was the venue that gave thousands of young boys and girls their first taste of education in South Longford. The author's sister Eithne (Bannon) kept a close eye on the new student.

THE FAMILY ... my parents 40th wedding anniversary was one of the rare occasions when the elders of the Mullooly clan gathered in 1986. Sadly all but one have now left us. Picture shows, back row, (l-r): Ivy Mullooly, (wife of Pee); Uncle Paddy Mullooly, Auntie Bridie Casey, Uncle Tommy Gilleran, Auntie Josie Lees, Uncle Jimmy Mullooly, Bill Lees, (husband of Josie). Front: Auntie Mary Mullooly, Uncle Pee Mullooly, my father, Dan, my mother Mollie and Auntie Eithne Gilleran.

After both working in the Longford and Cavan Leader newspapers Ciaran Mullooly and Angela O'Reilly were married on the 25th of May, 2000. Former colleagues in the papers and Shannonside radio produced a suitable front page headline to mark the occasion.

Albert Reynolds thought he was destined to fight the 1997 Presidential election for Fianna Fail. After playing his part in the peace process the Longford TD was confident of success but it was Mary McAleese who was ultimately chosen by the party to contest the poll. After her selection McAleese did an exhaustive media tour of the country.

After exposing the misdiagnosis of breast cancer among women at the Midland Regional Hospital in Portlaoise in 2007 the Author was the recipient of the Medical Journalist Of The Year Award. Awards compere, historian and broadcaster John Bowman stands in the wings.

Long before the fire, Cardinal Cahal Daly presided over dramatic changes to St. Mel's Cathedral in Longford in the 1970s when he was Bishop of Ardagh & Clonmacnoise. Shortly after his elevation, the new Primate of All Ireland came back to meet students (and the media) at the Athlone Institute of Technology. Norman Dungan was on sound and Neilius Dennehy shot the interview. Athlone printer Ciaran Temple, the AIT Board Chairman, listens carefully in the background.

He scored 137 goals for Manchester United in 361 appearances over eleven years but that is only half the story of the remarkable life and times of Belfast's George Best. After retirement he became a TV pundid and popped up everywhere on promotions and guests appearances, including the Shamrock Lodge hotel in Athlone before he died aged 59 in 2005.

Joe Farrell from Lisnacusha, Lanesborough was a man who loved horses all his life. A recognised expert in the field of draught mares he travelled the length and breath of Ireland to judge the breed at shows and events. He always said he would like to see the traditional horse fair of Lanesborough restored after it died out in the 1960s and in the 1990s his dream came through with the successful restaging of the event for hundreds of horse owners.

Shannonside Radio has proven to be a successful training school for dozens of broadcasters since it first went on air in Longford, Roscommon and South Leitrim in 1990. Disc Jockeys Peter Casey and Joe Finnegan were among a workforce of over thirty who took to the airwaves. When Niall Delaney moved to North West Radio in Sligo the author joined the station and presented the 'Mullooly At Mid-day' show.

FACE TO FACE ....David Kelly (l/r), son of Paddy Kelly , a former member of the Irish Defence Forces who was shot dead by members of the Provisional IRA in Derrada Woods, county Leitrim on December 16th, 1983 confronts Martin McGuinness, Sinn Fein Chief negotiator and Presidential candidate while canvassing in the Golden Island Shopping Centre, Athlone on October 10th, 2011. The confrontation was filmed by the author and RTE crewman Padraig Treacy. Pic Courtesy of Westmeath Independent

THE END OF THE LINE......former Government Minister Mary O'Rourke surrounded  by friends and supporters at the RTE outside broadcast point in the Community Centre, Kenagh while attending one of the many General Election counts in the Longford-Westmeath constituency. O'Rourke lost her seat to her running mate Donie Cassidy in 2002  but later returned to the Seanad to conclude an auspicious career in political life.

Restoring the number of young and mature coarse fishermen using the hot water stretch at Lanesborough is absolutely crucial. The 2015 International competition attracted 42 anglers from all over Britain and Ireland but the fishing is not what it used to be and the arrival of the invasive species of Asian Clams has the potential to do serious damage to the area if we are not alert to the threat. For years this hot water stretch was one of the most popular in Europe but its future is now unclear because of the presence of the Asian Clams, despite the staging of events for young and old in 2015.

The opening of the new Riverside Park in Ballyleague in May 2015 was the culmination of a lot of hard work by a great local committee. Picture shows the members of the Ballyleague Village Renewal and Tidy Towns Committee: (left to right) Gerry Trimble, Marie Burke, Margaret Thompson, Minister of State Michael Ring who did the opening, Councillor John Cummins, Chairman of Roscommon County Council, Detta Cox, Mary Greally, Joe Cribbin, James Hudson, John Francis Donlon, Fr John McManus, Vivian Young and John O'Loughlin.

Members of Ballyleague Mens Shed and tutors pictured with one of the traditional lake boats that they made in winter/spring 2014/2015. Picture: Andrew Fox

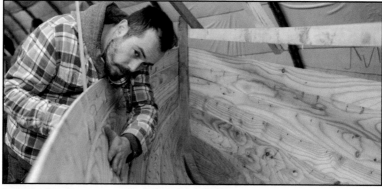

Jordan Estall working on one of the clinker style wooden boats in winter/spring 2014/2015. Picture: Andrew Fox

*From this ...*

The redevelopment of the
Riverside Park at Ballyleague,
Lanesboro, Co. Roscommon has
been an outstanding success
after a lot of hard work by local
volunteers.

*To this ...*

from his cigarette, giving him the aura (in the mind of a child anyway) of a John F. Kennedy iconic character here in the midst of our own small country town. It was real showbiz.

He had shown his cuteness from the very start. A friend of Joe Sheridan, the Independent TD who had represented Longford-Westmeath for many years, he appropriated many of his slogans and campaign tricks. 'Vote For Joe, The Man You Know', Sheridan had printed on his leaflets. Albert kept it equally simple when elected in 1977, promoting his personality over the party slogan at every given opportunity. The truth, of course, is that he also 'stole' the Fianna Fail seat held in the constituency by the late Frank Carter, surrounding the incumbent with his own new team of canvassers and supporters and effectively de-selecting him when nomination time came. A very decent man of social skill and immense popularity, Albert showed time after time in his career that he could be ruthless when required. Just as he did with Frank Carter in those early days, and with Charles Haughey a decade later, he equally demonstrated it several times over the years with his C&D Foods business and Fianna Fail political dealings.

I was thrilled to meet James Flanagan from Moate in the carpark outside the Sacred Heart Church in Donnybrook on the day Albert was buried. One of dozens who worked tirelessly for Reynolds Dancing Limited in the dancehall business days, he stood shoulder to shoulder with brothers Jim and Albert in the cash office, mineral bar and on the door for the opening of the dances in the 50's at the Roseland in Moate. When Albert's autobiography came out in 2008, James was in there among the leaders of the world, getting a very honourable mention from the great man who obviously cherished their friendship. It was appropriate then that Flanagan was at the funeral, once again among the rich and the famous, to remember his own old boss one more time, a man who did so much for rural Ireland in that era of dancehall music and ballrooms of romance. There too at the funeral was the great Dessie Hynes - a staunch friend of Albert's and a man who once ran a shop for his Aunt in Lanesborough before going on to mightier things in

O'Donoghue's of Merrion Row and a string of other successful bars throughout Dublin city. When Albert Reynolds first hit the Dáil floor in 1977, his star quickly soared. He may have been very busy at a national level with ministerial duties related to phones and industry and energy, but locally 'Albert' was still very much the man to get things done. This was the pragmatic politics of the 70's and 80's and, if you wanted something achieved, you headed to Longford and one of Reynolds' clinics in his Church Street office. I remember very well my own family making one such trip. A piece of land commission land had come up for distribution in our own area and my father, wanting to see if he could get a slice of it to add to the modest holding he already had, planned and executed the mission to see Albert. The office in Church Street was bland, probably one of the most boring little meeting rooms you ever came across, and Albert's sidekicks Mickey Doherty and Tom Donlon always took the message down very quickly and passed it on. The usual foray of letters with harps and acknowledgements then followed, before a phonecall from the man himself suggested the 'prize' would indeed follow. Unfortunately, in this case it did not materialise. I'm not sure whether it was the collapse of the Government or the deep recession of the 80's that put paid to the distribution of the land, but in the end it was let by an auctioneer in a public setting and we got it that way instead for a number of years, though Albert was never blamed by my father for what had happened.

It was another ten years before I met face to face with him, this time in very different circumstances. The tide of politics had now turned for the Rooskey man and he was Minister for Finance, second-most powerful in the Irish Government and riding high in the political game. Always affable and approachable to the media (perhaps this was part of his downfall), Albert never turned down an invitation in front of a microphone. When I came back from the Cavan Leader to become news editor at Shannonside Radio, he became a regular feature of my life. It is not surprising that most of the occasions that have stuck in the memory, however, from those days were social ones. I recall countless cups of tea and debates with him about when, and if, Charles Haughey would go. The phrase 'There is no vacancy" seemed to arise in every interview we did each Monday for months, but eventually Sean Doherty ensured that the green 'vacancy' light went on and we all hit the roadshow for Leinster House, Buswells and, critically, Jurys Towers Hotel. Shannonside Radio's new-kid-on-the-block was heading into the big league: senior championship hurling at last!

It was up there on the top floor of that D4 hotel that the 'Yellow Rose of Finglas', the late Jim Tunney and Chairman of the Fianna Fail parliamentary party, introduced Albert Reynolds publicly as the new leader of Fianna Fail. At a packed press conference, Albert made sure his local radio station was afforded the opportunity to ask a question at the top table. Two woefully-short years and ten cruelly short months followed when Longford became the media-capital each weekend Albert was home and we got the opportunity to question our very own Taoiseach on, not just the state of St. Joseph's Hospital, but the United Nations, the White House and anything else in the universe that was moving. It was simply a different world for us all.

After that, the return journeys to Rooskey and Longford were few and far between, with the bitter nature of Albert's political demise haunting the man for many years. But with lasting peace finally arriving up North, it has been very special to see the first chapters of his legacy being written in recent years. Twenty years after his resignation as Taoiseach, Albert Reynolds quite rightly got the plaudits he deserved the week that he died, and I know very well how proud he would have been of the brave words spoken by his daughter Miriam and his son Philip at his state funeral. They made sure he was not let down on his last day.

"Who is afraid of peace?" Albert famously asked the parties up North as he tried to patch together an agreement in the 90's. How much greater an epitaph could anybody have? Rest In Peace, Albert: your work is done.

Chapter 16

# FOOL ME ONCE

I was never a good man for going into hospitals. In fact, if truth were told, I hate the very thought of having to walk into any medical unit of any type, whether it be as a patient or simply as a visitor.

My distaste for accident and emergency and the environs of any of our local hospitals was firmly established after the sudden death of my brother on the 16th April 2000. On a quiet Sunday morning I rushed to the A&E unit of Mullingar General Hospital where he had taken ill, and I will never forget the traumatic hours that followed as Sunday morning became Sunday afternoon and Sunday evening became Sunday night in that hospital. Anybody who has experienced the sudden death of a loved one will not need reminding of the way this sort of ordeal scars you forever and a day, and today, like for so many others, that hospital ward smell of antiseptic and Jeyes fluid brings back the horrific images yet again within fractions of a second whenever I visit a hospital.

It may seem a little hypocritical then for me to say it but, for all of this personal baggage that I carry, it seems to me that it could be justifiably claimed that the people of Roscommon are not doing enough at the present time to stand up for their own hospital to ensure that it is not undermined or down-sized in the coming weeks and months as the recession continues to hit spending on health and all other areas. I know many feel strongly that the only way the people of the county can ensure the long term survival of their local hospital is to get into it and use it, increasing the throughput of the A&E unit and the various wards as time goes on and keeping it busier than it ever has been before. But if the hospital is to survive then it's also going to need a very influential 'political' wing , large volumes of public support, protest and a lot more legwork by a lot of people.

At the weekend more than eight hundred people marched through the streets of Ballinasloe amid fears that Portiuncula Hospital may be downgraded as part of a restructuring of hospitals in the region and it doesn't take a brain scientist to tell you that if Portiuncula is facing some sort of a change in regime then Roscommon cannot be far behind.

All the unions that represent the workers in Portiuncula and Roscommon have been making a very big deal in the last few weeks about the HSE's decision to expand the role of the new general manager at Galway University Hospitals to include Portiuncula and Roscommon. The union people say there is only one logical follow-on from such a move and that could result in the downgrading of the Ballinasloe and Roscommon facilities and see local services and jobs transferred to Galway but the HSE flatly denies this. Padraig Mulligan, the Western assistant general secretary of the trade union IMPACT, has been the front runner in making allegations about the HSE's real intentions. He told the march on Sunday in Ballinasloe that even though Roscommon and Portiuncula are both independent budget holders at the moment, that will change and they will be significantly disadvantaged if the new manager is sitting behind a desk in Galway City.

I am not really sure if Padraig's logic about the political motivation behind the changes really holds water but he is surely entitled to his view. He claims that Castlebar, which is the other western hospital that has been left out of this new management scenario, is enjoying special status because he believes there's a Taoiseach-in-waiting there. Despite this, he's hoping that the sway of public opinion will bring pressure on Brian Cowen and the HSE to ensure nothing changes in Ballinasloe or Roscommon in the weeks and months ahead. It is hard to know what influence Enda Kenny can really have already exerted on the HSE from his position as leader of the opposition and, in fact, some might argue that it would have been a lot more opportunistic of the HSE to move in now and downgrade Mayo's hospitals before any election.

Padraig Mulligan is right to point out the incredibly important value of the hospitals to the economy of the West, alongside the very serious health issues that go with their closure. I had reason to drive around Ballinasloe only last Thursday while waiting for a meeting in the area and Mulligan is speaking the truth when he says the town is a pale shadow of what it once was. I remember working as a reporter outside the gates of the Square D factory in Ballinasloe the day the last of the 200 jobs went there as it closed down. It was pretty devastating stuff for the dozens of women who had worked there most of their adult lives and they knew in their hearts that getting a replacement job in the same league would be a hopeless cause.

When you drive out the road and go past the now derelict AT Cross factory in the town the hair stands on your head. This mighty brand name, known all over the world, was responsible for some 250 jobs in its day but the plant in Ballinasloe is long closed and now looks so pathetic in its present derelict state with the huge logo still very evident. The third jewel in the crown for the horse fair town was very much the Dubarry shoe-making plant and, of course, that is also gone. All that remains is a management and marketing operation and a factory shop and God only knows what has became of the two hundred workers and their families who once relied on this giant for their income in the past.

For the people of Roscommon Town there should be warning bells ringing at almighty volumes as they read about the way Ballinasloe has already suffered. I am reliably told that ten more shops have closed down in the town this year. The district is a very serious black spot in relation to unemployment and one shudders to think what would happen if Portiuncula is indeed downgraded in the months to come.

The HSE's denial that the hospital is indeed being undermined is not a statement that leaves a great deal of confidence in its wake. "In the course of recruiting a new general manager for Galway University Hospitals a national decision has been taken to expand the role to include Portiuncula Hospital and Roscommon County Hospital," the statement said. "This decision has been made because of the need for greater integration of services for better and safer patient care, and to provide additional support to both hospitals."

Critics of the HSE will point out that greater integration of services in the past was simply a plan by the HSE to stop outside office hours surgery in Roscommon County Hospital. That move would really have meant the death knell for a fully functional acute hospital here and only the intervention of Mary Harney stopped that proposal from becoming a reality in Roscommon. It is hardly surprising that the public is again sceptical of any new plan to start expanding the role being played by a manager who would, at the end of the day, be in charge of two hospitals some eighty kilometres apart.

One other factor is worth mentioning in the wake of the weekend's protest in Ballinasloe. Now would be a good time, in the view of many of his constituents, for the Minister of State Michael Finneran to come out and do an extensive interview about the long term future of the county hospital in Roscommon, letting us know how he reads the present move to expand the role of the general manager, where the funding is going to come from for next year, and how strong the commitment really is at this point of the recession from Fianna Fail and his Government to the future of the county hospital?

*UPDATE: The accident and emergency unit closed down at Roscommon county hospital in the first week of July 2011 and all of the fears and concerns expressed in this column (written more than a year previously) were realised. In all my time covering news and current affairs in the county I have never seen anything like the fallout from the closure decision. The Taoiseach Enda Kenny was at the centre of much of the controversy - a pre-election promise about the hospital made outside Gleesons on the Square in* the town, coming back to haunt him in the weeks and months that followed and the Fine Gael party imploded when the A&E closed. Denis Naughten and Frank Feighan were at the centre of huge pressure and public protest. Naughten left the party in the end while Feighan, whose base is in Boyle much further away from the hospital, decided to stay and had to endure the most difficult of personal abuse. My strongest memories of the whole episode were not in Roscommon town at all but down in Monksland in Athlone on the day the Taoiseach visited Denis Naughten's new constituency offices - before the hospital closed. The protesters took over the car park outside the building and Kenny himself was the subject of sharp criticism as he tried to speak to them amidst the heckling. It was all a bit like watching a car crash as Kenny gave the first indication the hospital A&E was doomed and Naughten, by his side, realised he would soon have to make the biggest political decision of his career.

Today we only have what is known as an urgent care centre in Roscommon hospital during day time hours. It has its uses. I used it myself only in recent weeks for our son to be successfully given five or six stitches on a cut knee and, while there has been significant investment in the construction of a new endoscopy department at the hospital, the fact remains that an ambulance to Galway city is the only answer for somebody who needs critical emergency care, and that journey can still be too long for many.

One of the most despicable aspects of the whole closure debacle was the tactic used by some in the health area to tarnish the good name of the Dr Pat McHugh, the physician who had dedicated much of his life to the hospital. Claims that the mortality rate in Roscommon were way above other comparable acute units around the country subsequently never stood up and Dr McHugh went to his grave rightly aggrieved about what had been said.

The county hospital in Roscommon will always dominate the political debate in this region as a result of what happened in 2011. I have no doubt the future of the unit will make or break a few more political careers in the years to come, but nobody will be allowed to forget the events of 2010 and 2011 for some time to come.

Chapter 17

# THE AMBUSH

It was a misty, murky and grey December day in 1983 when an army private named Paddy Kelly from Moate, County Westmeath lost his life in a violent confrontation with members of a Provisional IRA gang in a wood near the town of Ballinamore in County Leitrim. Private Kelly, who was just thirty-five years old at the time, was married with four young children ranging in age from nine to just eleven weeks old, and was killed along with Garda recruit Gary Sheehan from Monaghan in what was effectively a shoot-out with the kidnappers of the businessman Don Tidey at Derrada Woods. Many questions still surround the incident and these violent deaths but, twenty five years later, nobody has been convicted before the courts in connection with either of these deaths and to say that it's an open sore on the face of the families involved and the defence forces in particular is to put it mildly.

Last Tuesday morning the people of Moate and the wider army community turned out in what could best be described as a remarkably similar misty, murky and grey day for the opening of a new children's playground and park built in honour of the dead solider near the old Clara Road junction in Moate. The park was being named after Paddy Kelly because he is the only Irish soldier to die in combat on home soil since the end of the Civil War and the top brass in the defence forces were not going to let the occasion pass without once again expressing their revulsion at what had happened to their fallen comrade all the way back in the early days of the 1980's. Brigadier General Gerry Hegarty, the general officer commanding the 4th Western Brigade with his HQ based in Athlone spoke loud and clear, eloquently telling his audience how proud he was of the soldier who died but went much further later by stating that many members of the Defence Forces who knew Private Kelly remained angry that nobody has been convicted of his murder. "Paddy was a much respected colleague. He was a real soldier and to have a soldier gunned down at home is a lot different to being murdered overseas," Brigadier General Hegarty said. "It was people like Paddy Kelly who defended this State when it needed defending against those bent on its destruction. Until somebody is held to account for that murder, we will still be angry about it. I think everybody knows who was responsible on that day and we would like to see somebody brought to account for it."

I must say that I was surprised when I heard Gerry Hegarty's words for the first time. Military events are usually notoriously stuffy affairs, normally staged with a huge emphasis on pomp and ceremony, and controversial comments like the ones spoken by Brigadier General Hegarty are rarely heard in these circumstances. I think it is indicative of the seething anger within the army that this senior officer should choose to use those words twenty five years after the events of Derrada Woods where two men had been killed as they tried to do their duty for their nation.

The businessman Don Tidey was also clearly emotionally affected by the day that was in it. He made a rare public appearance in Moate to lay a wreath at the memorial park dedicated to a soldier who died trying to protect him and he showed all his old military expertise when he stepped forward to salute the man who saved his life. Tidey is seventy three years old now but still a commanding figure of a man and only spoke during a court case this year for the first time about the scenes of chaos that followed the shootout in Ballinamore. It was really frightening stuff. He revealed that on his 23rd day in captivity in the woods his hood was removed and replaced with a balaclava and his legs were unchained. He said he only then became aware of noise and movement and he heard voices and the sound of dogs. There was then a burst of gunfire, then more gunfire. "Frankly from that moment on it became a battleground," he said in the Central Criminal Court while giving evidence during the trial of Maze prison escaper Brendan "Bik" McFarlane.

Mc Farlane (56), a father of three, of Jamaica Street in Belfast was arrested outside Dundalk and charged in January 1998. He had pleaded not guilty to falsely imprisoning Don Tidey and after a short trial was cleared of the kidnap of the former supermarket executive. That acquittal and the fact that nobody from any IRA gang has been convicted for their part in the deaths of Paddy Kelly and Gary Sheehan still clearly grates heavily on the army. Brendan McFarlane left the Four Courts an innocent man in the eyes of the law after the court had ruled as 'inadmissible' an alleged admission he made to Gardaí that he had been at the wood in County Leitrim where Mr Tidey was held captive. McFarlane's trial is over but for others the misery and trauma goes on.

Watching Paddy Kelly's widow Catriona speaking softly to Don Tidey at the memorial park in Moate last week was a fascinating experience. She was not only receptive to Mr Tidey's courtesy but very warm in her words about his treatment of her family and friends. "Mr Tidey is a gentleman," she told me afterwards and one by one she brought her sons around to shake his hands again as the mist began to fall in the memorial park. It really was a very strange day, one when you could feel all the raw emotion of an event a quarter of a century previously coming back into the atmosphere, a day when thoughts were clearly on others, taken away so savagely from their family and friends yet here in the middle of it all was a really striking exchange between two people who really looked like long-lost relatives.

The ceremony was attended by soldiers serving in the 4th Western Brigade and the Irish United Veterans Association, who honoured Private Kelly's three tours of duty with the United Nations. The Gardai were represented by Assistant Garda Commissioner Fintan Fanning, although members of the Sheehan family, who also lost a loved one, were not present. Afterwards a memorial Mass was held at the Carmelite church in the town. In the midst of the fading light in the park I chatted for a while to Paddy Cooney, the Minister for Defence during that entire episode so many years ago, who could clearly speak more proficiently than most about the pain of the army for their murdered colleague. He spoke of the deep shock at what had happened and the anguish of those who had actually seen the remains of Paddy Kelly in the immediate aftermath of his death. It was a shattering blow to one and all.

For the widow left behind life must also have been even more difficult. The Kellys emigrated to London two years later. Catriona, who was just 30 years old at the time of her husband's slaying, had to start again in a different land but clearly raised a very fine family and one that her late husband would certainly be very proud of. She now says she is hoping to return to Ireland to live and work and join her sons, David (34), Michael (31), Patrick (29) and Andrew (25) who have all returned home. Andrew has now followed his father into the army and only returned from duty in Chad recently. His brother David did most of the talking to the media and told me that the family were resigned to the belief that nobody would ever be held accountable for the crimes committed at Derrada Woods. "We have to draw a line under it. It looks like no one will ever be prosecuted for the murder of my father or the Garda recruit," he said.

Leaving the memorial park and walking back to my car in Moate on Tuesday I couldn't help but be affected by the emotion of it all. The anger, hurt and sadness that was felt by Paddy's comrades in 1983 clearly hasn't faded and there's a bitter resentment against those who harboured the gang responsible for the deaths and helped them avoid justice. "We cannot or will not forget the ultimate sacrifice Paddy Kelly made," Brigadier Gerry Hegarty said at the ceremony. Brigadier Hegarty and his many colleagues in the defence forces have done him a great service by the strength and forcefulness with which they marked the 25th anniversary of his death. His heroic service to the state is now set out and clearly established by their words and deeds. His memory will live on.

*UPDATE: We were not to know it that day but Private Paddy Kelly's son David was to not only honour his father's memory but play a much more significant and extraordinary role in public life in the months that followed that memorial park event in Moate. On Monday October 10th, 2011 the candidates in the Republic of Ireland Presidential election were all busy out canvassing around the country in the run up to Election Day. This was turning into one of the fiercest election contests in decades with the Labour candidate Michael D Higgins trailing in the polls behind the 48 year old businessman and entrepreneur Sean Gallagher, and my news duties on that day brought me to the Golden Island shopping centre in Athlone where one of the men who was next emerging as a front runner in the contest was about to meet the public.*

*Martin McGuinness has always denied being a member of the Provisional IRA's army council at the time when Paddy Kelly was shot dead in Ballinamore but from the heart of the busy crowds in the Golden Island shopping centre on that day a most extraordinary confrontation developed. I was just waiting around like everyone else for the Presidential candidate in the mall at the main door of the centre when*

*David Kelly pounced. Holding a framed photograph of his father, which
also contained Private Paddy Kelly's Defence Forces unit markings,
David Kelly moved in with army-like precision and immediately put
himself between the reporters present and Sinn Fein's chief negotiator :
"Martin McGuinness, hello, I'd like to ask you a question," he charged
with the TV camera now rolling beside him. "This is my father, Private
Patrick Kelly who was killed in Derrada Wood, Ballinamore, County
Leitrim in 1983 by the Provisional IRA. No-one has ever been prosecuted
for his murder and the murder of Garda Gary Sheehan, two brave
servants of this State. I want justice for my father, but I believe you know
the names of the killers of my father and I want you to tell me who they
are," Mr Kelly said, during a confrontation which was witnessed by a
posse of reporters and Sinn Fein supporters.*

*McGuinness was clearly taken aback by the incident but composed
himself as David Kelly spoke and then calmly responded by saying he
didn't know who the killers were. But the man from Moate was in no
mood to accept those words and countered by telling McGuinness he
was on the Army Council of the IRA at the time, which the Presidential
candidate denied. "I want justice for my father. I am his son. He was loyal
to this Irish Republic and I want to get justice for him," said David Kelly.
Mr McGuinness said he understood and sympathised with Mr Kelly,
but David then said he didn't believe him and called the presidential
hopeful a liar, which Mr McGuinness disputed. "I want justice for my
father. I want you to get your comrades who committed this crime to hand
themselves into the Gardai," said Mr Kelly.*

*The confronation was electric and seemed to go on for ages. As word
of the clash spread and more and more media people arrived my mobile
phone began to ring and my task was to try and get away from the
shopping centre and return to the RTE studios in the town to feed the
material to the lunchtime news bulletins. David Kelly wasn't finished.
"I want truth today. Murder is murder. I want justice for my father,"*

he charged as Mr McGuinness and his supporters moved away to canvas shoppers and workers in the shopping centre. "I asked him a direct question," David said to me on camera afterwards. " I wanted him to reveal the killers of my father and Garda Gary Sheehan. If they want a true peace process the truth has to come out before there can be reconciliation."

Asked how he felt when he first heard Mr McGuinness was running for president, Mr Kelly said, "Well, it's an obscenity because his organisation killed members of the security forces, my dad in the Irish Army. It's an obscenity. I feel sympathy for all people who were killed by the Provisional IRA over the years, Detective Garda Gerry McCabe in Limerick and all the other people." Mr Kelly, who said he had confronted Mr McGuinness on behalf of his family added, "I'd like to remember my father and my mother, whose life was ruined and she passed away early. There was a direct link between my father's death and hers. It destroyed her life, ruined her life." In another few moments he was gone. David Kelly slipped away quietly through the side doors of the mall in the Golden Island . He had achieved what he set out to do. Martin McGuinness continued his canvas but the story was out and was now about to go viral on social media and fill TV and radio bulletins for several days. The pictures went far beyond the Golden Island and Athlone that day. That night the BBC news brought the story to an international audience, and the day Martin McGuinness was ambushed as he tried to canvass for votes in an Athlone shopping centre would never be forgotten.

# CHAPTER 18

# THE POWER OF WIND

The convoy of lorries moved slowly along the roads of Offaly in the heart of night. Apart from the distant call of a bird on the Grand Canal, all was quiet as they travelled the Tullamore bypass towards the sleepy townland of Mountlucas, 21 kilometres away from the county town and even closer to Edenderry on the Kildare border. The first major industrial development targeted at this district for decades, their cargo was about to give this quiet corner of the midlands some of the tallest turbines in Ireland, a landmark feature to dominate for generations to come.

The Siemens brand on the lorries shouted out the code name for this complicated operation, a regular feature of life in the dark around here. For weeks, the new Bord na Mona windfarm at Mountlucas had moved 28 giant turbines onto the site by night, an operation planned to ensure as little disruption of traffic as possible but, under the cloak of darkness, a manoeuvre that also left some locals deeply cynical about the quiet but very definite manner their countryside was about to change. Of course the planning process for all this was transparent. Mountlucas was based entirely on a flat bog in an area where nobody in the community would have to live within 800 metres of the giant turbines if they didn't want to so this had been one of the less controversial developments to hit the radar and Bord na Mona seized the initiative to push on and draw up other plans along the same scale for locations elsewhere on their giant tracts of peatland.

I had carefully watched a debate about this divisive issue in my own native area when Coillte took on many in the local community to develop a windfarm on Sliabh Bán overlooking Ballyleague-Lanesborough. Keen to see just how big the turbines were, I wandered onto the windfarm site in Mountlucas a few times while it was being built to catch a glimpse of the extraordinary foundations for the tower stems and blades which would soon spin perpetually to create electricity here. It was a strange experience similar to early scenes in Jurassic Park driving a 4x4 jeep through the site from one giant hole in the bog into the next, tracing the route from one turbine to another, as if something quite colossal had just leaped out before us leaving extraordinary footprints for dozens of men to scurry around pile-driving and pouring concrete in its wake.

There were 28 gigantic holes in total throughout the bog, each seemingly capable of hiding a 747 jet. Whether agreeing or disagreeing with the principles behind these structures, Bord na Mona's first serious foray into wind farming in Offaly had been good for employment, the construction phase alone keeping young people at home and in gainful employment for months. Every day they travelled from Tipperary, Meath and elsewhere to these sites to prepare for the next turbine, the wooden frames pushed and pulled into position over a tangled web of steel that made the foundations even more secure for the Siemens equipment on the way. The development was also a bit like Christmas every day for the cement business in the region. On site one day, somebody told me that it takes more than €60,000 worth of cement to fill each and every foundation. That's a lot of dough for a business that has been in free-fall since the construction business crumbled.

The tragedy for the midlands is that the turbines themselves are not being made in Ireland. From a very early stage we were told it was neither practical nor viable for Siemens or any of the world's largest manufacturers to base a manufacturing facility here. Yet locals were given hope and fine words of encouragement at several high-profile conferences in Tullamore and elsewhere that there would be a knock-on effect from the arrival of thousands of the turbines for local industry. Jobs would be created in the manufacture of other components such as the blades and it would be a win-win situation for the people asked to live within sight of the giant propellers and watch their local landscape transformed for ever. It certainly hasn't materialised that way.

Portarlington was one of the towns that could have badly done with the boost. Once the proud home of the giant steel firm Butlers, 'Port' is nowadays feeling the crippling effect of the recession. Although the old Butler Steel site was once so vast and well-equipped that it could easily have provided a venue for turbine manufacturers, even at a different level, nothing happened and no such base was ever created. I asked John Reilly, Bord na Mona's head of power generation why couldn't industrialists of the region pull together, borrow the capital and build the plant when so many windfarms were being talked about? The answer, he said, was that the turbine manufacturers wanted to see definite business on their books before they forked out (you might call it 'concrete' evidence that the business would be there for them in the next ten years or so) and that meant they would want to see both the planning applications and the decisions made to allow these huge developments go-ahead, and we never really reached that stage in terms of scale.

So while the €120 million investment in Mountlucas was welcome, once the construction stage was over and the giant blades began to rotate, the number of new jobs created by this windfarm was no more than 60, many of them temporary. A far smaller number worked in ongoing maintenance and engineering, something critics of the project had pointed to as the biggest weakness of all, the toll of such a dramatic industrial development on the aesthetics of the Irish countryside without making any meaningful long-term impact on unemployment levels in the region. Eventually the turbine convoys in the middle of the night came to an end, the white Siemens brand name was raised slowly over each of those giant holes in the bog, and the project started to work. The tallest turbines in Ireland now soar over thousands of acres of bogland. Nothing will stop it now, but such cannot be said about the dozens of other windfarm projects behind it, all heading slowly towards the planning process. The lorries carrying these turbines have not yet been lined up in Dublin port, and we will have to see how they emerge once the new dawn has broken.

*UPDATE: As if there was any doubt about the company's long-term plans, Bord na Mona's new Managing Director, Mike Quinn, went on the record in October 2015 to say that wind energy and other alternative methods of electricity production were coming down the line and about to derail peat harvesting for ever. In an announcement that seemed to surprise unions, the company said the industrial scale exploitation of Ireland's bogs will have ended in 15 years, with the household briquette biting the dust for good. The company said it plans to transform itself into an alternative energy company, centred on biomass, wind and solar power, but Bord na Mona workers at Lough Ree Power in Lanesborough and West Offaly Power in Shannonbridge are still wondering exactly where the biomass might come from. As it stands, farmers here have shown little or no interest in growing either willow or elephant grass and, unless more incentives are forthcoming, it is hard to see the biomass coming from within the country at all. The 'Bord' has billed this as "the biggest change of use involving Irish land in modern history" and, according to Mike Quinn, are committed to opening a new windfarm every year for the next seven years. It is a huge target, and one that may well depend on the outcome of local planning concerns in many areas.*

*This represents a huge wake-up call for the people of the Midlands. We always knew that peat sources would be exhausted in due course but seeing the year 2030 going up in big print as the end date has already shaken quite a few communities. Deep down everyone knows that biomass and wind will never create as many jobs in the economy here as peat harvesting has done for over sixty years, so small towns and villages must now look elsewhere if they are to sustain rural communities.*

*Bord na Mona insists that much of their vast tracts of land across Kildare, Offaly, Westmeath, Longford and Roscommon – nearly 80,000 hectares in total – will be taken over by willow plantations, but others are not so sure. When the peat harvesting stops altogether on the larger bogs in 2030, a further 125,000 acres will be available for other uses and that's a scenario that will present even further challenges and opportunities to rural communities, a theme I will return to at the end of the book.*

# CHAPTER 19

# THE FLIGHT TO HELL

It was in fact originally called flight EI 234 and meant to bring a hundred and forty commuters on a relaxing weekend visit to Scotland. We queued that night in Dublin airport and watched in shock as a 7.00 pm flight originally became an 8.30 pm departure. The weather and an unexpected problem with an air traffic control computer was blamed for the delay. Everything would eventually be alright on the night, we were assured. 8.30 pm came and went and soon the monitor informed us 8.45 pm would be our new departing time: the walk through duty-free was a nervous one. The weather outside did look dodgy but at least we were on our way. 'Boarding now,' said the flashing monitor. I almost hugged it. On board, the usual preparations were underway, with flight attendants showing no obvious signs of distress as they advised us to look after our own oxygen in the "unlikely event of a sudden loss of cabin pressure." Seat belts were fastened, evening paper now open and ready for departure.

I still remember the fourth time the pilot came on the intercom. You tend to remember that little 'bing-bong' noise that precedes the sombre tone that threatens to dislocate your nerves with its frequency on nights like this. "There are unscheduled problems with the runway," the young man informed us. "It will take another fifteen minutes before clearance from the tower above us." No problem, we said. Weekend away. All night ahead of us. Duty free still open. Two papers left to read. It would, of course, eventually be alright on the night. The 10.30 pm 'bing-bong' was met with a chorus of sighs and nervous twitches. "We're returning to the terminal," said the pilot. "In the event of take-off, I am not satisfied that our brakes would be effective on the runway," said the man in charge of the plane. Reassuring, I thought, wondering if this guy had ever seen Airplane - The Movie.

Back in the departures hall that monitor of ours was still smirking: 'EI 234 next announcement – 11.45 pm' it pronounced. Frustration aside for a moment, we fled to the restaurant to seek relief. Closed, said the assistant. Last of the cheese sandwiches just gone, said the chef. I'm off home, said the cashier attendant. Me too, I wanted to say. At midnight, the flight to hell was cancelled. It was all pretty unsightly I am afraid. Yet again the departure monitor stole the show, changing the message of 'Next announcement at 11.45pm' to 'Flight cancelled', without even a shiver of embarrassment or apology. Beneath, however, absolute mayhem broke out. 140 people queued in the dead of night to interrogate a poor, defenceless Aer Lingus official who should have been canonised. "Where's our hotel?" some people charged. "What time will our flight leave in the morning?" others demanded. Okay, so the flight's cancelled. It will eventually be alright on the night. Won't it? Tell me it will be ... please? "EI Flight 234 was not the first flight cancelled tonight," said the Aer Lingus official, still angling his body nervously away from the customer service desk in order to avoid the possibility of knives being used. "Unfortunately we have already placed all the other customers in the available hotel rooms: you will have to sleep here for the night." By the time all the verbals died down between St Eamonn of Aer Lingus and the most aggrieved of the customers, the fainthearted were already waving the white flag. An elderly lady was already dozing on a nearby bench, a few hours' sleep her only alternative on a night of horror.

12.50 am and only 20 people remain ahead of us in the queue to talk to St Eamonn. A change of flight will be sought, an extra night in Glasgow perhaps, so it eventually might even be alright on the additional night. Enter the Airport Police. Waking customers who were already sleeping and pointing torches at others, they informed passengers we would have to move. "Security measures," they insisted. The elderly lady looked like she was about to have a stroke. Slowly but surely we were all marched back down from the boarding area to the luxurious main hall of Dublin airport. For the carriers of duty-free, there was to be another treat of having bottles confiscated as we left the boarding area. Another fourteen scuffles broke out, in words. At this stage we were all just desperate. "Wake me up," I said to my long-suffering fiance. "It's all a nightmare." Well it wasn't and next morning, after a sleepless night on a rock-hard Dublin airport seat, we did indeed fly to Glasgow. The weekend, or what was left of it, was extended by Aer Lingus for one extra night. The air hostess on board apologised until she was quite blue in the face and today a nice letter from the customer relations department in the airline did it all over again. Free travel vouchers or a full refund was the letter's final offer. No excuse was even proferred.

It was in many ways a trying experience for everyone. An incident like this reminds you from time to time that things can wrong, and they certainly did. Let's just say I am trying to be tolerant about it all. Nobody died and I am sure everyone in the airline tried their best but, put it this way, we won't be looking back on our visit to Glasgow for many weeks to come. And I can't say I feel an urge to invest in Aer Lingus either at the moment. It could all have been so different, if only everything had been alright on the night.

*UPDATE: I find it all just a little embarrassing reading back on this old column. In retrospect, I have come to the opinion this was the first ever experience I must have had of a properly delayed flight, and when I look at the old Champion newspaper cutting in which it was published I am even more mortified. On that particular week the editor had decided to give the column to a cartoonist, so accompanying the piece was a very fetching image of yours truly sitting in the departure lounge of the airport with a small, elderly man resting his weary head on my shoulder. The caption read, "Thank you, son: will you hold my false teeth please?"*

*Fortunately the memory of that long night at the airport is well and truly erased now. The opening of Knock Airport with daily flights in and out of the UK has transformed my life as an airport user. In the last two years, I don't believe I have been in Dublin airport more than twice as the handy trip to Mayo replaced the long haul to the capital. Even today with the motorway network having shortened the trip, I still prefer to slip down to Strokestown from Roscommon and onward to Ballaghdareen, where access to Knock Airport is so convenient and hassle-free: it's a 55 minute journey to heaven. There's something so very reassuring about parking your car within a hundred yards of an airport and walking into a departure area without miles and miles of security-checking queues, and our family have become major fans of Knock. Today the airport authorities have erected a life-size statue on the approach road to the terminal of the great man who built it, and every time we pass it we still sing his praises. If only we had more visionaries like Canon Horan on this small island.*

*I am not sure if you have ever spent a night trying to sleep on an airport seat but, if you did, you will appreciate just how 'narky' the writer was when he penned the original article. That experience must be up there with anyone ever forced to try and kip for the night in a car after a music festival or a late night out, and I have unfortunately done that too. But that's another story ...*

# Chapter 20

# SUPER MAC

I sat beside Bernard McNamara a few years ago during a social function in the Innis Ree Nursing Home in Ballyleague. He struck me as a quiet-spoken and remarkably modest man who didn't really fit the sort of description that goes with the perception we normally have of big-shot builders and developers. He wasn't loud or gregarious, didn't have a helicopter (at least not on that day as far as I could see), and talked a lot of common sense as we enjoyed our lunch.

If memory serves me right, Mr McNamara was one of the investors who actually set up Ballyleague's nursing home and a handful of others around the country around the same time, subsequently selling his interest on and no doubt making a very decent profit. When Ballyleague's was built and ready to open I think it was called something like the 'First Citizen Residential Centre' and they had a type of an open-day for locals to come in and see where they might choose to enjoy their retirement when the time comes. It was a community event and was very well supported: it was also very informal.

During the course of the half hour that it took us to eat the food on the table, the conversation turned to a few different issues. Mr McNamara remained polite and thought-provoking at all times but had a clear and very definite fix on the financial implications of what he was involved in. I also remember him slagging my good wife when she revealed to him that she was a Cavan woman. "You are the ones that should be looking after the nation's money," he proclaimed, and we all laughed.

Last Wednesday evening I was driving back from Dublin when I heard the dulcet tones of Mr Bernard McNamara again, only this time in staggeringly different circumstances. In an emotional interview with RTE's Mary Wilson on the Drivetime Show on Radio 1, he admitted that he was broke, insisting that Michael McNamara & Company was a legally separate and profitable entity unaffected by the High Court judgment. He said property developers were now pariahs, but said he was not ashamed of anything he had done. "I will be there if they want to come and get me," he said. It was a highly charged interview and presenter Mary Wilson was certainly not giving the Clare businessman an easy ride.

My first reaction was one of some surprise that the developer had chosen at all to come on air to explain his situation: it was certainly not something that Liam Carroll or any of the other failed business icons of recent times had done following their day in court. It provided an amazing insight into what is going on in the boardrooms of the nation's big builders as the fallout continues from the annihilation of the construction sector and offered a glimpse of his contrasting style with those of his competitors in the business. It slowly became clear that there were very good legal and political reasons for him giving the interview in the first place: Mr McNamara's family home, purchased back in 1998 for €2.95m, is also at risk because of his present troubles. The house at 22 Ailesbury Road, Dublin 4, is registered in the name of Bernard and his wife Moira McNamara, according to the Registry of Deeds office. As charges and counterclaims flowed in the course of the next twenty five minutes or so, I couldn't help but think of where he had come from, what he had achieved before his commercial downfall, and how many jobs he had actually helped to create – even in Ballyleague – during his heyday in business.

McNamara's story is a real David and Goliath tale. He took the small building company founded by his father Michael in County Clare onto the national stage. Unlike other construction companies who started out as bricklayers, his background was fairly comfortable. In the recession-hit 1970s his father bought a house in Raglan Road in Dublin for £34,000 to accommodate his children going to college. It was a good investment.

The young Bernard McNamara left St Flannan's in Ennis with a few honours in his Leaving Cert and a clear ability to fend for himself. He was quickly encouraged by his father to study business in Dublin. In 1971, he joined his father's business, persuaded back down from Dublin to help out on three big contracts which had just been landed. Then his father's company got its biggest commission to date, building an extension to Galway hospital, and other health-board contracts followed. From there on they seemed to never look back.

The heir to the throne certainly pulled his weight in the expansion of the company from this time onwards. Bernard McNamara started an aggressive drive to win contracts and in 1984 moved to Dublin where he rolled up his sleeves and talked to the right people about new deals. In an interview for a book a few years ago, he admitted that he also got a taste for the Dublin social scene where real business was sometimes done in places like the Shelbourne Hotel. "When I came to Dublin I found I knew an awful lot of people I had met at Renvyle House in Connemara, where I had gone on holidays for 12 years," he said in that interview, "In Renvyle, I had not known what they did, but years later I found they were in businesses related to my own. I met more architects socially, whose office doors I could not get past, in the Shelbourne Bar with Moira on a Friday evening than any marketing guy going out knocking on doors." Now armed with a better contact book, Bernard McNamara led his father's company to new heights and within months the company went on to win several huge contracts for hospitals, public buildings and offices across the country. The McNamara name with those banner colours of Clare alongside have adorned building sites the length and breath of the land, and they're still there today.

So where did it all go wrong for Bernard McNamara? How could a bright and intelligent businessman, who became such as a star in the big league, not see just how fickle the business had become? Was he really so 'punch-drunk' in the Dublin 4 social scene that he didn't realise the train was now in 'run-away mode' without a driver and the next bend could bring such a paralysing derailment? In the RTE Radio Interview on Wednesday Mary Wison reminded him of the sign in Joe McHugh's pub in Liscannor, Co Clare (where he came from), as summing up what he learned in life. "Experience is what you get when you didn't get what you wanted," the sign says. "I certain got it now!" Mr McNamara said.

In 2005 Bernard McNamara's company turned over €360m, according to their accounts. He had a portfolio that encompassed student accommodation, nursing homes, landmark office blocks, apartments and large hotels. He built the National Gallery's Millennium wing and was responsible for the major development of St Vincent's Hospital. With his partner, Jerry O'Reilly, he bought the Galway Radisson, the Kilkenny Ormonde and the Parknasilla Hotel in Co Kerry, as well as the Tara Towers in Dublin 4. He then, as part of a part of another consortium, bought the Shelbourne Hotel for crazy money, and perhaps that was the first sign that he had indeed gone too far.

Today Bernard McNamara is reported to have left the country for a short holiday in Spain as he awaits a queue of people seeking their money back in various different banks at home here in Dublin. His future is most unclear but, for all of his critics, what he has achieved in terms of creating employment and building communities around the country cannot be taken away from him. At least in that respect he knows that his name will not be forgotten.

*UPDATE: Bernard McNamara is back in the construction business in Ireland and successfully building new developments in the capital city.*

Chapter 21

# SUFFER LITTLE CHILDREN

"They feel guilty. They feel they did something wrong. I can assure them that they did not." These were the measured and considerate words of Judge Miriam Reynolds at Roscommon Circuit Court last Thursday afternoon as she turned to the children abused and neglected by their forty year old mother and brought to an end, what I could only describe as the most stomach-churning two days of a court hearing that I have ever had to attend.

Sitting in the courthouse for more than six hours at this sentencing session was absolutely horrific – and that was only for me – a complete bystander in the case with no connection to the accused or her family. Can you even begin to start to try and understand how the woman's eldest son felt as he sat through it all? High above his mother's head in the public gallery when evidence was being given, he tried his best to take in the detail of the case and the facts as outlined by Garda Sergeant John Hynes, but at various stages over the two days you could see that the strain was taking a painful effect on him and indeed on his aunt who had acted so caringly and responsibly when she first reported her concerns about her sister's treatment of her family to the local GP.

Notwithstanding all the criticism and the other issues that have been raised since the seven year prison sentence was handed down last Thursday at ten minutes to one, I think we must make time this week to ensure that these people get the credit they deserve for the role they played in finally ending the ordeal for the six children involved. It could not have been easy for a woman to go and report her own sister to the authorities but she clearly saw the scale of the neglect that was involved and knew she had to do something for the welfare of the children. For the boys themselves to have to open up and try and tell their foster parents and the Gardai what had been done to them, it must have been extraordinarily difficult and painful but, once it was done, they surely felt that a huge weight had been taken off their shoulders.

Those who know something about child abuse cases that have already gone before the courts would argue that it is not surprising that few, if any, of the family's neighbours or relations really knew anything about the sexual abuse that was going on in the so-called 'house of horrors'. The widespread neglect of the children, the head lice, the damaged hair and the smells were all giveaway signs of children from a large family who were simply not been looked after but it would have been difficult, if not impossible, for anybody to have known at that stage without any further investigation that this woman was sexually assaulting her own son, unless the children had been taken into care at an earlier stage and it is undoubtedly unfair to hammer the locals for their failure to spot evidence of this unspeakable sexual abuse. We know from other appalling cases that have gone though the courts that this level of abuse usually exists in a culture of secrecy or silence and there can be no doubt that forty year old woman was well able to keep it that way and had already threatened her poor innocent children not to tell anybody.

The role of the HSE and the old health board in this entire situation is a different matter, however, and now something that will be the subject of an inquiry over the next number of weeks and months. When the court heard that social workers were called in as far back as 1996 to look into the neglect of the children in the family there were eye brows raised everywhere and, even though health chiefs tried to take the children into care in 2000, a serious amount of questions remain that will have to be answered. We heard last week the offences took place at the family's three-bedroom bungalow which was dirty, strewn with rubbish, cold, damp and had dead rats and mice inside and out. This was the house that the social workers and the childcare workers and the home helps were sent out to by the HSE and it is inconceivable that they would not have developed major concerns about all other issues way above and beyond the neglect factor as they went into that house every day. In an interview with Gardaí in 2006, the mother admitted that her children were often blue with the cold, only had dinner twice a week and had lice crawling around their heads and bodies, yet it appears that those who were charged with their care, and would have seen it up close, did not use enough of the powers that were available to them to forcefully remove those kids from the family home for once and for all. "Any possibility of them having a normal and proper life has been stolen from them by this woman who called herself their mother," the judge said on Thursday and that's the saddest part of all about everything that happened. While the prosecution is over and their mother starts her jail sentence, they are still facing the unbelievable task of trying to get their lives into some sort of shape or what the rest of us might call 'normal'. The hurt and damage caused to them throughout this eight year period means that all of the principles of their life to date are upside down. What they perceived to be right is now known to be very very wrong and they must be searching for answers on every single day they get out of bed, even with the best efforts of their foster parents to try and smooth the way for them.

The children were aged between just six and fifteen years of age when the offences took place. Shocking victim impact statements from them all were read to the court, detailing how they were not fed properly, their clothes were not washed and the range which heated the home was only lit once a month. I listened with absolute horror to each account of the damage that had been done and wondered when and where it would end. Their mother's defence for her actions was quite pathetic. We learned that she suffered from depression and asthma and has a drink problem, would routinely go to a pub in the evening at around 6pm, leaving the children alone, only returning home when she was drunk in the early hours of the morning, one of her sons said. In court we also heard the amazing story of how the children would often be let out of a school bus to join them at a pub in the evening – another unbelievable aspect of the story.

I know that last week's reporting of the case, and the high profile coverage it got, has shaken a lot of people's confidence in the childcare monitoring system we operate here and, for that reason, there is a need to move quickly to deal with these issues in a thorough investigation. Long delays, such as the ones experienced while following up inquiries in Monageer and in the Midland breast cancer misdiagnosis scandal, only serve to heighten fears among the public that people are afraid to see the truth coming out and strengthen the perception that a cover-up is possible if something is left back long enough. Unless firm action is taken you can bet that the same horrible thing could happen again, and that's the real lesson to be learned from the sad events of the last ten days.

*UPDATE: The 45-year old woman, who described herself as the 'worst mother in the world' walked free from the Dochas Women's Centre at Mountjoy Prison just before 10.30am on April 22nd, 2014. She had been jailed for the maximum term of seven years after becoming the first woman in Ireland to be convicted of incest but had a quarter of her sentence reduced for good behaviour. She was assaulted a number of times in prison while serving out her time for the crimes of incest, other sexual abuse, neglect and wilful ill-treatment of her six children. The house where she lived with her family had been dubbed by the print media as the House of Horrors.*

*What we couldn't report at the time of her trial was that the convicted woman's husband was also facing a trial, and was later convicted in 2010 for the systematic sexual abuse of his eldest son over a three-year period. The 57 year old man had pleaded not guilty to 47 counts of the rape and sexual assault of his son, when the boy was aged between 12 and 15 years old but, after his wife and son both gave evidence against him, was found* guilty and sentenced to 14 years in jail. Despite being found guilty by a jury, he continued to claim that he was innocent, appealed against the severity of the sentence and had it reduced by a higher court to 11 years.

There was a subsequent inquiry into the way the state responded to the events in the 'house of horrors' and, in a final report issued in October 2010, it concluded that, had there been a better insight and understanding of the condition and the needs of the children over a protracted period of time, the hope that this family could function in a positive way would have given way to serious concerns years earlier than it did and the children offered protection. The report also found that important child protection concerns were not addressed adequately over a number of years. This failure meant that the harm and neglect of the children and young adults in the family continued.

The inquiry team said the voices of the six children were not heard in this case. By not hearing directly the concerns of the children, the services could not respond fully to their needs, the report said. On October 27th, 2010 the HSE issued an "unreserved and unequivocal" apology to the six children involved in the Roscommon child abuse case. It said it accepted in full the findings and recommendations of the inquiry team, which identified major service failures by the then Western Health Board (later merged into the HSE) up to the time the children were taken into care in 2004. Recommendations for important changes were made, and did subsequently take place.

The six children in the family received support and assistance from relatives, friends and the HSE in the aftermath of the horrific ordeal they suffered. Four of them stayed in care for some time. The inquiry team said they had settled well in secure and caring foster homes and were progressing well. The two other children, who are now adults, subsequently lived with relatives as they tried to get on with the rest of their lives.

Judge Miriam Reynolds, who presided at the mother's court appearance and was highly praised for the way she conducted the hearing, subsequently took ill just months after the case ended and died on Friday March 20th, 2009.

# Chapter 22

# HOLDING OUT HOPE

My mother suffered from dementia following a stroke and was diagnosed as having a form of Alzheimer's disease about eight years before she died. She was a proud woman with a history of having bettered herself and her family through education and worked extremely hard for the good of her family throughout her life time, both before her marriage and afterwards. She was also a very caring person who loved the community in which she lived and treasured her roots in south Longford.

In the days before it became almost politically incorrect to use the term you could say that Mollie Mullooly was a 'housewife.' I suppose she would say first and foremost that she was a 'homemaker' but before she married she worked in the hotel and catering sector and would often entertain us with stories of her exploits down in Cork on Model Farm Road while training and after college on placement and at work in places like Bangor in Northern Ireland where she made many friends in the hotel sector. Having married a farmer and worked hard in rearing a family of six children she retired in her sixties and was both happy and even proud to receive her state pension for the first time. 'The winkin' as she jokingly referred to it gave her a financial independence that she never really had before that, an experience that most women of her time could certainly identify with. In retirement she also took up the game of bridge and enjoyed ten good years in the company of some really great friends in Lanesborough and Ballyleague, but it was after she suffered the stroke that she began to suffer acutely from memory loss and dementia.

I suppose, in retrospect, we all could claim that we had seen it coming. It was the small things firstly but when you are looking after six children, and a plethora of grandchildren that followed, it is normal for the woman of the house to be faced with certain 'memory-testing issues" from time to time. In my mother's case it was her trusted handbag that became the first real victim of her poor memory, the place where she hoarded everything and anything that she wanted to keep out of the reach of her marauding grandchildren or indeed her own sons and daughters for that matter. She kept sweets there first and foremost. She hid personal items too such as jewellery and contact information, her medical card and, almost daily for 20 years, she would leave her personal medication in the same place, usually well out of the way of the rest of the family and safely hidden. The problem was that over the years my mother has hidden her bag so well in our country home that not even she herself could eventually find it when the time came for its recovery and its urgent use and then pandemonium broke loose. I remember her losing her bag, or more correctly, forgetting where she had hidden it on at least twenty occasions when she was between 60 and 70 years old. Even though there was little thought about it at the time, I suppose we would now probably agree that it was one of the very early signs of the Alzheimer's disease that would tarnish her life so much in later years.

The truth was that in the aftermath of the stroke on that sunny summer's morning my mother's memory was never the same. After an initial period of rehabilitation she returned home but with her co-ordination very badly shaken. I remember driving her back to the house where she was born one Christmas day and watching her memory play tricks with her as she rocked between her days in school there and the time when she later married. "I have left the bike in the village," she told me with absolute sincerity in her eyes as we neared their home place, "I will pick it up there." The damage already done to her memory was now deeply distressing but very obviously permanent. Whether it was the stroke, the dementia or the form of Alzheimer's that she was later cared for, my mother's cognitive features were now in freefall and within a very short period of time she needed full-time care and attention. At this point in our lives the Alzheimer's Society of Ireland entered the fray and a local woman, who will never be forgotten for her care and consideration, introduced us to a whole team of new people who could care for my mother in a way that was especially considerate at all times. We were also fortunate that my late brother Pat was able to recruit a local woman to act as a loyal home help and, with the support of some other very considerate local nurses and her best friend and sister-in-law Mary Mullooly who lived next door, our mother enjoyed the remainder of her life in the company of several women who treated her as if she was their own kith and kin. We were so lucky to have such a team of fantastic people in our home and for their beautiful care and attention we will always be thankful.

I told the above story recently at Hannon's Hotel in Roscommon when I was asked to speak at the launch of details for the new Western Alzheimer's Respite centre planned for Tulsk in County Roscommon. Casting aside my own concerns about the personal nature of this story, I tried to explain to those present how valuable respite care would surely be to all those who had to tend for a loved one and reminded the audience that, while our mother was elderly for most of the illness, there were other carers that I met at the Alzheimer Society meetings who were looking after a much younger loved one, a person who often required a much higher level of care and supervision. I also made the point to the audience that there was a very real danger of Alzheimer's disease being responsible for two victims in a household instead of one, if the person doing the caring on a 24 hour basis was not given the support and help they required and the respite they so obviously needed from time to time. This I know from experience.

Alzheimer's is a horrible disease – perhaps the worst that can afflict our elderly, the one that we all fear deep down, but the respite centre that this new group of ambitious volunteers is trying to build in Tulsk has the potential to reduce the suffering and the pain for both those directly affected by the disease and their carers. I commend the project to one and all and pray that their new centre will go ahead in the near future with all of our support to make for a better life for hundreds of others in the years to come.

*UPDATE: It's five years since I sat in Hannon's Hotel in Roscommon and told a gathering about my mother's illness. I was there to support a small group of fiercely-determined and very genuine Roscommon volunteers who were really pushing the dream of having their own residential centre in Tulsk, and for months they worked very hard to try and achieve their goal. It had been explained to me several times that building the new centre would only be one of the challenges ahead of them, staffing it would be an entirely different affair and I think everyone in the room that day knew it was not going to be easy. The local committee really put in a super-human effort over many months gathering funds for the centre and in the end I believe that over a hundred thousand euro was collected to try and advance the project. I have to confess that for some time I heard little or nothing by way of an update about the initiative so, in the run up to the publication of this book, I endeavoured to try and find out what had happened to it.*

*I put a call into the Western Alzheimer's office in Roscommon town* who were very polite in dealing with my query. "Following changes in HIQA regulations coupled with the economic downturn the proposed unit is no longer viable and the group is currently re-evaluating the project," a very short statement confirmed, and I am afraid my heart fell on hearing the news. This is bitterly disappointing news for all those who helped that effort. I have no doubt that the recession has had a severe effect on this great project and, like a lot of other people, I hope that it may one day soon come to fruition. I am sure the money raised is in safe-keeping and that those responsible will try and make that dream come through in the not too distant future.

In the meantime the battle goes on for Alzheimer's sufferers and their families all over the world. In July of 2015 more hopes of some sort of a medical breakthrough in dealing with the illness surfaced after the publication of research by British and Canadian scientists. Experiments on mice indicated that a new vaccine not only halts the advance of the disease, but repairs damage already done. We were told later it could also be given to patients whose families have a history of Alzheimer's to prevent them developing the disease. And yet all the time this revolting illness spreads. A growing number of elderly and even middle-aged people are being struck down by the degenerative brain disease, which has some 500,000 sufferers in Britain and Ireland alone. We all know It causes untold misery to families who are left to care for loved ones who may no longer recognise them, and some of us who have been through the experience still wonder if there is not a better way to honour the lasting memory of somebody very close to them.

Chapter 23

# THE MIRACLE

When a raging fire gutted the interior of St. Mel's Cathedral in Longford town on Christmas day in 2009, some of the country's most priceless artefacts were burned to cinders. It was devastating. Included among the casualties was most of the 1000 year old wooden crozier of St. Mel, the saint who gave his name to this neo-classical style building that had its foundation stone laid in 1840. The devastating fire broke out in a chimney flue in the cathedral's dated heating system some time between midnight mass and five o clock in the morning and, according to locals, temperatures of up to 1100 degrees celsius were recorded as the blaze spread dramatically from under a wooden floor to the height of the beams and into the roof over the church.

The damage was catastrophic. The cathedral roof was gone, the floor had collapsed into the crypt, and so intense was the heat that marble fittings had melted. Paintings, tapestries and statues in that section were immediately destroyed, yet just a few yards from the epicentre of the blaze one remarkable painting was to survive the roaring fire. A work of art that was hanging on a wall at an altar in a side-aisle remained relatively unscathed by the inferno all around it and miraculously survived the fire largely intact. The painting of the holy family was not a masterpiece of 18th or 19th century art by any standards. Of Italian origin, it arrived in St. Mel's without much recognition for a little-known European artist and stood alone in the left aisle nearest the prayer offertory. A favourite of local churchgoers, it should have been one of the first canvasses likely to be set alight according to Ronan Moore, the senior project manager who helped guide St. Mel's back to full health. "We will never know how it survived," Ronan recalled in 'The Longford Phoenix' - the RTE documentary on the restoration of St. Mel's we produced for the cathedral's re-opening. "You can see it here just a few yards from some of the huge stone pillars and columns of the old church that were completely destablised by the searing heat of the fire, turning to dust and had to be replaced, yet the painting stayed intact above it all while all around it was destroyed by those huge temperatures."

He doesn't use the word lightly but the former Bishop of Ardagh and Clonmacnoise, Dr Colm O'Reilly has described the survival of the holy family painting to me as a miracle. On a cold and miserable winter's evening in late November 2014, as he prepared to re-enter St. Mel's to get his first sight of the painting since its return to the now-restored cathedral, he repeated his view that it was indeed miraculous that it should not have been completely destroyed while all around it perished on December 25th, 2009. Bishop Colm has now retired from active duty in the diocese. Aged 73 when the fire happened, he stood outside the burning church accepting handshakes and warm embraces from parishioners in the frosty conditions like a man who had just lost a loved one in death. "It was an horrendous experience to watch it dying before my eyes," he told me, "but one thing was clear even at that stage - it was impossible to save it."

Spending €30 million on the renovation of a church in the heart of the country's worst-ever recession was surely a decision he could never have taken were it not for the insurance coverage that St. Mel's enjoyed. In our RTE documentary, the former Bishop admitted that it would have been difficult to contemplate such a project ever being taken on at a time while one in five of the Longford population was out of work. Yet he is adamant that, insurance coverage aside, he also held the responsibility of a modern generation to ensure that one of the most important heritage buildings of the midlands was restored.

The engineering struggle involved in bringing St. Mel's back to its former glory was of titanic proportions. At one stage locals feared the building core would actually collapse because of the initial damage caused by the fire. The heart of the battle was to try and replace twenty-six gigantic limestone pillars lining the central aisles of the old cathedral. "We had to painstakingly remove and replace every one of them with new stone," Ronan Moore recalled. "This was one of the most challenging pieces of work I have ever had to take on, when one considers that all those stone columns stood eight metres high, each one consisting of a decorative capital, a fillet stone, four intermediate drums and a base, and weighed something like five tonnes apiece."

Given that there was no floor, no roof and that the 26 hand-carved limestone columns which supported the structure were effectively destroyed, the main building contractor Gem Purcell devised a system allowing the delicate restoration work to proceed on multiple levels at the same time. "We effectively had three building sites, one above the other," Martin Healy, managing director of Gem says. With no floor to support scaffolding, a suspended steel support 'bridge' was constructed to allow one team work on the roof while below the delicate task of replacing the columns continued alongside the 'defrassing' of the fire-damaged internal masonry walls. Meanwhile a concrete floor was laid while a team of highly-skilled plasterers set about recreating traditional cornices in the basement under master plasterer George O'Malley's supervision. And, above all of this, a new steel structure provided a temporary roof to keep the rain away and prevent further damage to the old cathedral. The quarrying project required to rebuild St. Mel's was mammoth, with over 675 tonnes of native blue limestone from Leighlin, Co Carlow, being installed for columns, hand-carved window surrounds, pilasters, and replacement corbels for the bell tower which also sustained some damage. To get this amount of limestone in the section sizes required, a staggering 10,400 tons had to be quarried.

Ronan Moore's 'Grand Designs' project was not without its setbacks. The sudden death in December 2011 of the chief architect Dr Richard Hurley was a huge blow and one that remarkably mirrored a similar event nearly two hundred years earlier when Joseph B Keane the original architect had also passed away while St. Mel's was being first built.

There were days in the filming of our documentary when the sheer scale of the carnage made it seem this old building could never be brought back to life, but what has emerged is a very different church in my eyes. Gone is the austere feel to the place, the long cold aisles leading down to the altar where my father brought me to attend confessions on many an icy Christmas Eve in the 80's, to be replaced today with a building that has a very modern feel, a newly designed sanctuary very much embracing the congregation and much closer to them in a physical way. It's not an accidental change of focus either. Dr Colm O'Reilly spoke in the documentary of the need to not just renew the old building in Longford but, after all the sexual abuse scandals and difficulties faced, to revive the church itself with its people. "We wanted to build a church that was a fitting and modern place for people to gather for prayer," he said, "but it goes far beyond that. Let this be a symbol somehow of renewal of the entire church in Ireland, a new cathedral for a different time."

*UPDATE: In a career spanning 21 years on TV, 'The Longford Phoenix' was one of the most personally rewarding pieces of television I have ever been involved with. It was an idea born out of a conversation with the cathedral administrator Fr. Tom Healy. From the earliest days, Tom could see the public interest in the restoration and, though slightly apprehensive about cameras, was keen to see the process properly recorded. Following the builders' and then-bishop Colm O'Reilly's agreement, I was directed to RTE's religious affairs department where I met with producer and photographer Birthe Tonseth. The subsequent three-year adventure involved numerous visits back and forth to Longford to see the milestones fall into place, as well as a personal trip down memory lane. When it was all over, the interior looked very different to churchgoers with seats for 200 people removed, a development that told its own story in the struggle for the faith. However, the pride of a county in the midst of this crippling recession was very much evident throughout and, when the Cathedral was officially reopened, they came from every corner in the country to see it. In the first 10 months a remarkable 100,000 visitors was recorded and the new bishop of Ardagh and Clonmacnoise Francis Duffy was good enough to acknowledge the role the documentary played in spreading that word. We were honoured and privileged to be there to record this important piece of living history, watched on television by over half a million people at home and abroad, showing a county and its people who have turned to their church for support and faith in some of the darkest days of the last decade but are now walking tall again as they rise up the steps under that famous portico to welcome back the spirit of St. Mel.*

# EPILOGUE

There's an important economic context for the book you've just read, and it's a very sobering one. Lanesborough - Ballyleague, where I live, has just experienced the full ravages of its first real full-on recession in the last five decades, and the pain has been all the more severe as a direct result. Like many other areas around the country this small town has also been hit with derelict buildings and closed-down businesses for nearly a decade. It's a wretched sight and has been soul-destroying to watch. There's also an eerie feel to the place, especially on week days, a sense that a whole generation of young people are missing from these streets and from the public waterways, those between 17 and 28 years of age lost through emigration.

There's a perfectly scientific reason why the people of the area have suffered more than most in this recession. During previous national economic slowdowns, our community relied heavily on two key industries in the heart of the town. The ESB and Bord na Mona employed more than a thousand people for many years, so we were relatively insulated from the worst of those national financial restrictions. In the 50's and 60's these two industries brought hundreds of people to work the bogs, set up new homes and bolster the business community in the town. For the most part they paid good wages. In the 90's while others struggled we were watching hundreds of jobs being created again by visiting construction firms as a new unit was built onto the old power-station. Even in the new millennium, while others experienced only modest growth our community once again was thriving after a decision to invest €250 million in a new peat-burning power station on a greenfield site. It is true that many of the construction workers this time came from Turkey and other places abroad, and were not always treated properly by their employers, but they ate, drank and stayed locally and once again the economy of the town benefited. I am not saying there was no emigration through these decades in this Shannonside town. Of course there was. Dozens left, many of them in the class I went to school with, but my point is that it could have been a hell of a lot worse, and for the most part it was a hell of a lot better than most other rural towns around the country. We certainly had our emigration but nothing on the scale as places like Kiltimagh, Belmullet or Drumshanbo, to name but three other rural western outposts.

You could argue that, like other 'energy' towns in the midlands, Lanesborough developed a culture of 'dependency' over the course of these five decades, and that was not a good thing either. Every Thursday and Friday evening the Bord na Mona and ESB workers left their jobs and presented themselves at the local pubs and shops to cash their pay cheques. There was no need for fancy marketing by any business in the town those days, no need even for food to be served in a bar because the same people kept coming back in week after week to hand over their wages and let the bar owners take a slice of the action and they knew they could depend on them. At the same time the fishermen came here from abroad week after week to get a taste of the hot water stretch without as much a tenner being spent by the locals on promotion in the early days. It was all one way traffic and the local business community, with only one or two honorable exceptions, became very much apathetic to anything else. They never had to search for the income like other towns did, there was never any need for any hunger to be shown. For that, the town suffered. While our shops and pubs had a steady trade without a lot of energy in the 1970s and the 1980s, other towns were standing up for themselves and growing an indigenous front. Smaller towns west of the Shannon were learning the business of self-helping. Co-operatives were set up to attract real tourists. Businesses and shops forged together to print brochures and build community and enterprise centres. Many smaller towns attracted business people to build new hotels and leisure facilities. They had to do it because they had no choice any other way: they could not depend on the local trade in the days of deep recession. There were no Bord na Mona cheques there. It is against this background that Ballyleague, Lanesborough and the surrounding areas felt the severest pain throughout this most lethal of recessions in 2009. Today ESB employ less than 40 people in Lanesborough, Bord na Mona have less than 250 on their books, and the people of our area have had to embrace the challenge of the new environment in which they live. In truth, we have had to stand up and get the finger out for the first time.

The response of the community has been very positive. The area where I live is an example to parishes all over the country that real progress can be made when people pool together. Yet so much more still remains to be done and has yet to be even started. The volunteers behind Lanesborough Tourism Co-op, Ballyleague Village Renewal and Cloontuskert Residents Association have led the way, with an attack on the asthetics of the area that is a real sight to behold. In my day job I drive thousands of miles every month through villages and towns all over the country, yet none of them have the entrance road landscaping that Lanesborough Tourism Co-op has installed on the Ballymahon road into the town and most of them could only dream of such a class act. In my youth away back in the early 80's the county council bought the land alongside this road as part of a plan to widen the main thoroughfare but for years the new lay-by just sat there deserted in a state of total dereliction and became the sight of dumping, decay and neglect. Seadha Ryan, Des McDermott, Bernadette Clancy, Vinny McGowan, Fabian Walshe and their colleagues (past and present) in the Tourism Co-op have dramatically changed all of that and a real beauty has indeed been born. With a team of committed FAS workers John L. Farrell executed the plan and today an avenue of beautiful trees line the route for at least a mile from the east into the town. A neat walking trail alongside the trees has proven to be one of the most popular leisure pursuits in the area and the route is always maintained impeccably by the FAS lads. I cannot think of any other town in Ireland that has such an inviting and attractive sight on its outskirts - a real avenue effect. Borrisokane in county Tipperary has what you might call a more mature version on its Nenagh Road, but even that seems poorly landscaped and thought out when compared to the Ballymahon road project. Throughout the town, the other work done by the Tourism Co-op has been exceptional. The walking trail through the woods in Commons North is a real revelation to passing visitors, perhaps taken too much for granted by locals. On a fine day it is a haven for wildlife and the flora and fauna is breathtaking. I believe this development has never been given the credit it deserved by the National Tidy Towns adjudicators either. The interpretative signage is first class and around the rest of the town there are simple but subtle touches by the same committee that have led to vast improvements. They really should take a bow.

Ballyleague's journey into the same league has been equally effective. In the 70's and 80's Frank Curley and others began the hard work of organising a development committee. A strong village renewal effort came along in the 90's with real progress made on street landscapes and a new push in the 'Noughties' has really seen the area shine. I was lucky enough to be part of a team of volunteers that has transformed the side of the river's edge , north of the bridge from a flooded grassy bank to a five star new cobble-locked promenade in the period between 2010 and 2015. The attention to detail has been meticulous and, from the day chairman James Hudson and his crew first visited a similar project down at Cortober near Carrick-on-Shannon on a fact-finding mission in 2011, I always knew this project would be done properly and with a touch of class. Today the stainless-steel railings and the ornate stonework at the entrance to the park gives a sense of great pride of place. Additional important renewal projects have been completed by the enthusiastic Joe Cribbin from Daybreak and others in the committee throughout the village in the last 5 years, not least the re-thatching of Mairtin's cottage at the Sliabh Ban hotel, a picture postcard that sets the theme for any visitor entering the town by car or by boat.

Cloontuskert's challenge was a very different one, but one they have also mastered with some prestige. A Bord na Mona designed housing development, this community has grown up and older since its formative early days. As people passed on or moved away the estate's demographic has also changed, yet the consistency with which they approached the aesthetics of the village is outstanding. Hard work and huge effort by people like Mary Murphy, Sean Carty and their neighbours was already rewarded by the National Tidy Towns competition adjudicators with medal-winning performances over a decade ago. A new energy has taken to the streets and the campus of the 'Abbey' again in recent times, which has not just produced a beautiful new orchard on what was barren land, but a new positivity for this community. Vinny Healy leads the team nowadays, but he would be the first to say he has several hard working commandos from the estate right behind him pushing him all the way.

All of these volunteers are unsung heroes in my eyes. They never look for credit and plaudits. They do it because they love where they live and I believe every parish in the country has similar heroes. In most areas it's a question of people with different skills and abilities working together to achieve a goal, a team of individuals with contrasting powers combining to make their area special and there is no reason why your own village or town should be any different.

Yet for all of the improvements that have already taken place on ether side of the Shannon in Lanesborough and Ballyleague, this is really only the start of the fightback for any country town in 2015. Changing the look of the place is one thing, changing the attitude inside people's minds is quite a different matter. The 'culture of dependency' is the issue that has made the renewal of small industry and the business of the town all the more difficult to get underway, but there are certainly signs of improvement and I am heartened already by some of the changes proposed. The closure of the Lough Ree Arms hotel was a body blow. Every town needs a small hotel, a place for somebody to not only get a bed while enjoying a short stay, but also sit down for a while, meet friends, conduct business and network with locals. Losing the Sliabh Ban Hotel was also a disaster for the area. Like many, I attended the function room there for celebrations, fundraisers, training events, tourism events and so much more. Its loss to the area was immense and the economic downturn that followed the sale will take a very long time to remedy the environment in which it could ever operate successfully again.

So what is to be done to kick-start the renewal that business and community needs so badly in towns like Ballyleague and Lanesborough? How can the town recover and try and get back to the lofty days of the 80's and 90's? Where can one start? Here's just a few ideas to contemplate.

I believe the fightback is already under way. Commitment and perseverance are the key ingredients. Encouraged by all of those aesthetic changes carried out already, some business people and entrepreneurs have already voted with confidence in the community and taken the first step to rebuild the town's commerce to its full potential. Chris and Marina Webb's decision to buy the old Convent of Mercy building near the river was a crucial beginning. Efforts have been successful in recent months to try and get the angling business off the floor. Over 40 visitors from the UK and further afield were brought in for a coarse fishing event in May 2015 and a world championship event with 14 participating countries is now scheduled to come to the town and Lough Ree in October 2016. Yet without proper accommodation available locally, the area will never capitalise on this sort of tourism product. In the same way, events such as the very successful Tri Lanesborough Two Provinces Triathlon and the Lough Ree Environmental Summer School bring dozens of people into the community every year, but only for a day trip because they have sought and failed to get a B & B for the night convenient to the town centre. Having met with Chris and Marina I believe that the crucial first issue of providing proper accommodation for visitors is now about to be tackled in the former Convent of Mercy building. This couple has worked hard to renovate the building and develop different models of accommodation on-site. They tell me they will offer bed and breakfast, self-catering accommodation and perhaps even short- to medium-term stays at the heart of the town centre and this is really tremendous news. They also underline the fact they need proper broadband to develop the business and there are indications that the national network will extend itself properly to the town in early 2016 and this is absolutely crucial. Too many small towns in the midlands have been left behind while broadband bounces through the streets of our major cities and the new initiatives planned for rural Ireland cannot happen quickly enough.

While the Webbs have been planning a future for one building along the main artery of Lanesborough, the Brehon family have taken the bull by the horns and bought the old Lough Ree Arms hotel with plans for further development. This hostelry was renowned for its hospitality for fishermen in the 70's and 80's (see separate chapter) and I believe it can also contribute in a huge way to the renewal of the area. Knowing the calibre of the family who bought it, I am confident that the new Lough Ree Arms will fulfill all those demands we place nowadays on the hospitality sector in a modern society.

Across the water in Ballyleague there are also some signs of a recovery and the renewal of the community. When Ray's Filling Station closed on the Roscommon Road at Ballyclare many of us lamented the fact the first sight facing the incoming traffic into the village was that of a closed-down business. Ray was immensely popular and had worked hard for Ballyleague, so news that John James Greene from Newtowncashel, another young man full of energy, had bought the site in recent times was warmly welcome. When I spoke to the new owner on the phone in Australia recently I was greatly encouraged with his own vision for the future of the property and the transformation he has in mind in the coming months and years. I think I can safely say that he will give Ballyleague the sort of 'gateway' presence it really needs on such a great lay-by approaching the town, and the sooner the better.

These three property transactions are really important. They give us all real evidence that there is a confidence out there for the future of the area. Other projects such as the re-development of Kelly's old post office building at the entrance to Lanesborough car park will also enhance the visitor experience here, but the businesses that are already open and have served the town well for generations have also a crucial part to play in the fightback. The story of the closure of the Northern Bank in Lanesborough is a good example of how we can turn a negative development into a real shot in the arm for the commerce of the town. I was more annoyed than anyone when National Irish Bank decided to pull the plug and walk away. In the early days of the new millennium I worked with a small team of local business concerns who went into the bank and tried to push and shove them towards opening an ATM machine outside the branch, offering greater support from the local commerce industry in turn for a relatively small investment that would give tourists and locals alike the sort of convenience to cash that is absolutely essential in any modern town. At that stage there was no ATM in Lanesborough. At first there was huge resistance to the move. The bank officials said their ownership was changing, the branch was not big enough and there were all sorts of security issues alongside other excuses. Week by week locals lobbied the management at Belfast level and eventually they give in. There was a sense that it was easier to concede in the end than fight the good fight as they saw it. The new machine brought a welcome boost to the economy of the town. In those days very few gave cash back on a card transaction in a local shop or pub, so not having to go to Roscommon or Longford for an ATM machine was certainly a great addition, especially if you were on a boat on the Shannon passing through town. Business definitely benefited. The news that NIB were walking away was really a sickening blow. There were a few efforts made to change the bank's minds but the national trend for NIB was to get out of doing face-to-face business with human beings in small towns any more and that's what they were determined to do. Councillor Mark Casey and his colleagues, to their credit, did pursue the bank on the ATM machine issue and, even though it was also pulled out within hours of the bank closing, a replacement site was eventually secured at the SuperValu store across the road and, thanks to Bernard Keane, the service is still there and very busy today.

The closure was followed by the usual predictions of doom. A town without a bank is a town without commerce, we were told time and time again and there was no doubt that for some businesses who need access to cash and change it was a horrible blow. When one local family stepped forward to later try and buy the bank from NIB the whole story was about to be turned on its head. Today Gareth Johnston's pharmacy operate a very successful business in the exact same room where once the Northern bank tellers did their thing with popular local services such as Keri's Beauty-room and the Health Bank on site. On a recent visit I even noticed that the same front door is in operation and there's a great energy and a business feel to the place. Gareth Johnston and his family obviously bought the building for sound commercial reasons, but his decision to set up the pharmacy and health bank here is a huge vote of confidence in the local economy. The O'Brien family has also served the area so very well over several generations in their own pharmacy in town but competition is the heart of all business life and

Lanesborough needed that element at play so very badly. Suddenly the loss of NIB is not such a loss after all, and the contribution played by Gareth and his team is growing all the time. From the depths of despair you can certainly say something quite inspirational really emerged.

Lanesborough needed a second pharmacy in the same way in which Ballyleague needs a second pub. I grew up at a time when Harold's Shannon Bar was thriving under the management of Martin Leckey and his wife Anne Marie Harold. If the truth were to be told, I regularly frequented the snug at the back of the bar and enjoyed many · a celebration there, so when the pub closed in later years I saw it as a huge loss to the wider Ballyleague/Lanesborough area. In our days growing up, customers moved their money between the two pubs in Ballyleague on a regular basis throughout any night of business. Of course you had some who were regular customers with the late Charlie and Julia Sorohan or the Shannon Bar, but the younger audience who contributed most to the profits at the weekends had a much more transient behavioural mood. We played pool in Sorohan's and snooker on the new table in the back of Harold's. Then when Sorohan's got the snooker room we moved back there to become Denis Taylor and Steve Davis but still watched the football in Harold's and darts was also very popular there. Many years later when I returned from Dublin to work in the midlands I couldn't believe that Harold's bar was closed. I was genuinely sorry to see the doors locked because I felt it was an important if not crucial contributor to the economy of Ballyleague and I still believe that today. Such was my confidence in the place that I even wrote to the owner John Gordon Harold in the USA and offered to buy the pub at one stage and give Mike Sorohan a new neighbour across the road. Sometimes I am happy he decided not to sell it as the bar trade went through a much tougher time after that, but on other occasions when I see the lonely nature of the street in the village and the absence of cars outside the premises I am not so happy. I wanted to buy Harold's, turn it partially into a restaurant of the style of Keenans in Tarmonbarry with a view of the Shannon behind it and give locals and visitors the quality of food that one now expects. At that stage there were no restaurants at all open in the town and there was a crying demand for it after five years of very successful summer schools and festivals, but my offer was politely declined and I returned to the day job, much to my wife's relief I think. When Paul Horohoe decided to open his 'PS Red' restaurant across the road in Sorohans in October 2015 the area finally got the high quality á la carte restuarant it needed - albeit fifteen years later.

Today I am pleased to report there are several venues where quality food can indeed be attained in my home town and the place where I live. The Sister's Bistro, The Swan Tavern and PS Red at The Lifebelt all serve different markets and it is a real pleasure to tell somebody who has just got off a cruiser in the marina in Ballyleague in search of a plate of grub about the variety that is available. Throw in a very comprehensive deli operation at Supervalu and Spar, a Chinese takeaway and two chip shops, and you can see we have come a long way in sorting out this particular demand from visitors. What we need now is a consistency for the customer and an ongoing push to raise the bar even higher, as has been done successfully in places such as Tarmonbarry and Glasson, but the local community must also play their part by supporting these businesses with their custom.

Providing a warm bed for the night and a proper dinner are just two basic enough opening demands that any modern town in Ireland has to face in its battle for business. Renewing the commerce of the rest of the town will be the next difficult part of the journey. Tourism is a crucial player in the midlands. I passionately believe that a new state of the art water sports, tourism and angling centre is the next step that has to be taken to give the area a constant business line that will continue long into the Autumn after the cruisers have left and can even take up residence in the area all year round, if properly designed and constituted. The arrival of Center Parcs in Ballymahon could be the catalyst for this important development to be kick-started. When operational, this new forest village at Newcastle woods will attract thousands of people every week in search of Ireland's first tropical world swimming complex and some forty out-door pursuits. We are reliably informed that these visiting families pay heavily for their four-day and three-days trips into the complex in the woods, but it seems to me that, when the tourists leave Ballymahon on the Thursday evening after their four-day stay, there is a very real opportunity for Ballyleague and Lanesborough, Roscommon, Longford, Athlone, Mullingar (and other areas nearby) to cash in on a business opportunity and try and offer an additional 3-day holiday break for a percentage of the families to really enjoy over what's left of their weekend. A high-quality water sports and outdoor pursuits venue just fifteen minutes away, equipped with proper accommodation and competitively priced, would surely encourage some to stay on. What is needed at this stage to make this happen are people with vision, a plan for investment, a cohesive marketing strategy and experience in what they are trying to do. I am glad to say that a few locals and people from outside the community have already opened their eyes to the possibilities that Center Parcs will offer. In recent months I have spoken to business interests who would like to open a new wake-boarding attraction on the Shannon, also offering local boat hire, bike hire, canoeing and kayaking and much more to school tours and others. The spin off for the area would be fantastic and present the sort of '9 months a year attraction' that the business community needs to justify the sort of investments required. So how will it happen or, more importantly, who will make it happen?

The answer to that question is … ourselves. The residents of the beautiful riverside town and village of Ballyleague and Lanesborough are ultimately the people with the power to decide their own fate. We have proven in the past that we can rise to that challenge and meet the community demands. There never has been a better time to start - with the EU Leader programme on the way back and supporting rural tourism development. We have also some of the finest GAA grounds to be found anywhere in the country, new schools and facilities, more clubs and organisations than some counties can even dream of and, above all, we have the will to make things happen. I don't think there's any real doubt about that. In the course of helping my neighbours in Ballyleague prepare some statistics for the visit by the judges in the National Pride of Place competition in September 2015 I researched, compiled and costed a factual list of developments kick-started west of the bridge and effectively put into operation by the will of the people there. The money invested is, in the language of people of the USA, awesome and solid proof of what can be achieved. The community engaged time and time again with public and state bodies to make a long lasting difference for youth, the elderly, people with special needs and tourists, showing an incredible inwards investment of up to €10 million in the parish of Kilgefin alone in under 10 years.

It all began in 2005 with the development of the new marina in Ballyleague, proposed by Ballyleague Village renewal committee carried out by Roscommon county council, Waterways Ireland and Central Government and costing €2 million. In 2005 and 2008, the progress continued with the opening of the new school in Cloontuskert and school extensions at Ballyleague, carried out by the school boards of management with the assistance of the parents associations, local fundraising and the Department of Education. Each school is now equipped with facilities for students with special needs and have the services of Special Needs Assistants and the money raised was over €1.5 million. The previously mentioned re-development of Ballyleague Riverside Park with new quayside wall, promenade and angling facilities for the disabled was carried out by Ballyleague Village Renewal committee in association with Roscommon county council, Tourism Ireland, Inland Fisheries Ireland, Waterways Ireland , Supervalu and ESB at a cost of €400,000. Between 2007 and 2015, the development of St. Faithleach's GAA club grounds, club house, dressing rooms and pitches was also carried out with the support of the local community, the GAA, the National Lottery, Sports Capital Grant aid and central government to the tune of another €1.5 Million. It really is a staggering set of achievements in a relatively short space of time.

All of this development is publicly-funded and when you consider that in the same period the private sector came on board with the development of two state of the art nursing home facilities for the elderly in Ballyleague at Innis Ree and Costellos, (which are also continuously supported by local community and employing local people) you begin to see the real will that already exists when it comes to people pushing on and developing their own area. It seems to me, without taking a microscope to the parish, Lanesborough has shown equal prowess in lobbying and drawing down public funds in the same period with over €1 million spent on the new fire station alone just last year and new developments at the GAA grounds, the community college and in the other schools. So what does all this prove? It shows an undoubted ability of the people of this community to get up of their posteriors when the need is great and operate the political system to get what they want from central Government. It also shows, through the local contributions, that people will form fundraising committees, run draws and events and raise their own fair share: we will stand up and be counted, and we can do it when we want to. The culture of dependency is long gone, you could argue.

I suggest that the key to successful re-development of the commerce and business of any rural community requires high quantities of commitment, perseverance, energy and enthusiasm. In the coming years we will need all the experience and good will of the volunteers in Lanesborough Tourism, Cloontuskert residents committee and the Ballyleague village renewal group to achieve more. We will also need the passive section of the local community to come on board and roll up their sleeves to make it happen. Renewing Lanesborough, Ballyleague, Cloontuskert and everywhere else is about taking steps to ensure that our children, the next generation, have a town where they can live and work in years to come. It's about ensuring there will be summer jobs for teenagers and students, proper seasonal positions for part time farmers and high quality well paid permanent positions for those who would like to stay here and raise a family here.

It's not rocket science either. ESB and Bord na Mona have both a valuable part to play in the economic regeneration of the area and the sooner everybody sits down and draws up a plan to get that renewal under way the better. Some people have already shown the vision and have started to come up with ideas. Joe O'Brien is one such person. When the ESB closed down Ferbane power station and walked away they left behind a community fund of over €1 Million for Offaly county council to administer in the setting up of a new community business park. I have been in it many times, and it is a relative success in that there are still a number of people employed in several units, including a playschool and a printing firm that relocated there from elsewhere in the village. But there are lessons to be learned too about how this can be done in our own community and the process of adapting that model for what we will have left here long after the ESB has gone for good. Bord na Mona's stated ambition to be out of the peat harvesting game in 2030 presents the biggest challenge of all to midlands communities - who must now wake up and prepare a timeline to provide alternative job creation projects.

The coming months will present the ESB, Bord na Mona and everyone else in this community with challenges to roll up their sleeves and plan for Lanesborough and Ballyleague and towns like them in the year 2020 and beyond. Some will stand up and play their role, the rest will leave it to others to shape the future. Let's hope you and the members of your family will take your destiny in your own hands and seize the moment.

# REFERENCES

1. **Death Of A Way Of Life -** published for the first time, November 2015

2. **Memories of St. Mel's -** edited copy of original version for the 'Mel's Review ' Christmas edition, Parish of Templemichael in the Diocese of Ardagh & Clonmacnoise at December 2010

3. **Reelin' In The Years -** edited version of original article published in the Roscommon Champion, October 7th, 2008

4. **Say Hello - Wave Goodbye -** edited version of original article published in the Roscommon Champion, August 11th, 2009

5. **The Day The Music Died -** edited version of original article published in the Roscommon Champion, September 9th, 2008

6. **Here Is The News -** edited version of original article published in the Roscommon Champion, December 16th, 2008

7. **When the Party Stops -** edited version of original article published in the Roscommon Champion, September 30th, 2008

8. **Postcard from America -** edited version of original article published in the Roscommon Champion, October 28th, 2008

9. **The Big Freeze -** edited version of original article published in the Roscommon Champion, January 12th, 2010

10. **Praying for St. Anthonys -** edited version of original article published in the Roscommon Champion, August 10th, 2010

11. **You're On Air -** edited version of original article published in the Roscommon Champion, December 1st, 2009

12. **The Man from Clare -** Edited version of original article in July

of 2010 and published at the time in the Roscommon Champion newspaper. Ciaran Mullooly was a student at Lanesborough Vocational school from September 1979 and June 1984

**13. Letter to Eoghan -** edited version of original article published in the Roscommon Champion, December 8th, 2009

**14. The Cruelty of Nature -** edited version of original article published in the Roscommon Champion, April 27th, 2010

**15. Local Hero -** edited version of original article published in the Roscommon People, 28th August , 2014

**16. Fool Me Once -** edited version of original article published in the Roscommon Champion, March 16th, 2010

**17. The Ambush -** edited version of original article published in the Roscommon Champion, Tuesday December 16th, 2008

**18. The Power of Wind -** edited version of an original blog for the RTE News website posted on February 3rd, 2014

**19. The Flight To Hell -** edited version of an original article published in the Roscommon Champion, Tuesday 24th February 1998

**20. Super Mac -** edited version of an original article published in the Roscommon Champion, January 20th, 2008

**21. Suffer The Little Children -** edited version of an original article published in the Roscommon Champion, January 27th, 2009

**22. Holding Out Hope -** edited version of original article published in the Roscommon Champion, February 3rd, 2009

**23. The Miracle -** edited version of original article published in the Irish Daily Mail, Monday December 15th, 2014

# AFTERWORD

My unique 'journey' as a journalist has taken me to a wide variety of places all over Ireland and abroad over the course of the last 25 years. I have met with and reported on tragedy, death, destruction and despair, alongside a fair share of more positive and upbeat stories along the way, and taken great hope and inspiration from many of those whom I have encountered. Throughout most of that time I also wrote a weekly column in the Roscommon Champion provincial newspaper and thoroughly enjoyed the opportunity to offer the type of additional insights and opinions that a ninety second TV or radio report could never compete with. When the Champion closed I made a personal oath to friends and family I would someday publish a select share of those columns from the best part of 20 years in print and put them on the permanent record. Finally that opportunity has arrived.

When I sat down to edit the original pieces and update them for the benefit of readers I also realised that I had to take out the laptop and write some more, fill in the gaps so to speak, on my own fifty years on this earth, enlighten the reader on the great changes I have seen in that time and perhaps give a context for many of the strong views held. I have also returned to my roots in the Shannonside twin towns of Ballyleague and Lanesborough, cast an eye further on the media and events elsewhere in the midlands and invited you the reader to look ahead at the many challenges we all face. This is not just a book about the R word. Recession certainly dominates many chapters but I also hope the new ideas and suggestions I have made will prove somewhat of a catalyst for two more Rs in the coming years, recovery and renewal in our society.

I want to thank my neighbour Aine Keenan for patiently guiding me along the road from an archive to a successful manuscript. I say thanks to Fiona Healy of the Roscommon People for assisting me in the layout and design process and Andrew Fox, Anne Hennessy, Nicolette Spellic and Kip Carroll for providing us with visual images. Sincere thanks also to Frank Quinn, Derrick Turner and Turners Printing Company for their professionalism and to Kevin Bakhurst for the encouragement to make the St. Mel's documentary and finally finish this book!

To my wife Angela and my sons Bryan and Eoghan I reserve the greatest of praise. Thank you all for putting up with this cranky author in his 50th year, prompting me with some great suggestions for my weekly columns through all that time, double-guessing some of my wandering ideas on writing and helping me to get a second book to the printers. I hope you will agree - it's all been worthwhile.